Song of Solomon

Love Is Strong as Death

Love is strong as death, jealousy is fierce as the grave.
Its flashes are flashes of fire, the very flame of the LORD.

Song of Solomon 8:6

By Gary Dunker

CONCORDIA PUBLISHING HOUSE · SAINT LOUIS

3558 S. Jefferson Ave., St. Louis, MO 63118-3968
1-800-325-3040 • www.cph.org

Written by Gary Dunker

Edited by Robert C. Baker

This publication may be available in braille, in large print, or on cassette tape for the visually impaired. Please allow 8 to 12 weeks for delivery. Write to the Library for the Blind, 7550 Watson Rd., St. Louis, MO 63119-4409; call toll-free 1-888-215-2455; or visit the Web site: www.blindmission.org.

Manufactured in the United States of America

1 2 3 4 5 6 7 8 9 10 15 14 13 12 11 10 09 08 07 06

Contents

History	*Date (BC)*	*Solomon*
	ca. 1010	Saul and Jonathan are killed; David begins reign (2 Samuel 5:4)
		Solomon, second son of David and Bathsheba, born (2 Samuel 12:24)
Iberians invade modern Spain; Mayan dynasties founded in Central America	1000	
	970	David dies and Solomon ascends to the throne (1 Kings 2:10–12)
	960	Solomon begins building palace and the Jerusalem temple (1 Kings 6:1)
Pharaoh Psusennes rules Egypt	959–945	Solomon marries Pharaoh's daughter and builds her a house (1 Kings 7:8)
	953–947	Temple completed after seven years (1 Kings 6:38), Solomon's palace after thirteen years (7:1)
		Solomon writes portions of *Proverbs* (1:1; 10:1; 25:1); *Song of Solomon* (1:1); and *Ecclesiastes* (1:1, 12, 16)
Pharaoh Shishak I begins rule in Egypt	945	
	930	Solomon dies (1 Kings 11:42–43); kingdom divides into North and South (12:16–24)

An Outline of Song of Solomon

Nestled amid the pages of the Old Testament sits a seldom-read book, Song of Solomon. God's Old Testament people considered Song of Solomon a simultaneous recounting of the love of Solomon and the Shulammite (perhaps Abishag the Shulammite referenced in 1 Kings 1 and 2) *and* a retelling of God's love for His bride whom He wed in Exodus. For early Christians, the Song's countermelody, the love theme of Solomon and the Shulammite, plays softly in the foreground while the dramatic theme of Christ's love for His Church, His betrothed virgin bride, plays triumphantly in the background.

Any outline of Song of Solomon must focus on the oft-repeated theme of love; a love springing from heavenly origins is the "flame of the LORD" (8:6).

- I. Cycle One (1:1–17)
  - A. Introducing the Author (1:1)
  - B. Longing for Kisses (1:2–4)
  - C. The Vineyard and the Shepherd (1:5–8)
  - D. The Bride Adorned (1:9–17)
- II. Cycle Two (2:1–17)
  - A. The Lily and the Apple Tree (2:1–7)
  - B. A Spring Marriage Proposal (2:8–17)
- III. Cycle Three (3:1–4:7)
  - A. First Nocturnal Search (3:1–5)
  - B. The Wedding Procession (3:6–11)
  - C. The Flawless Bride (4:1–7)
- IV. Cycle Four (4:8–5:1)
  - A. Edenic Garden (4:8–11)
  - B. Living Waters (4:12–5:1)
- V. Cycle Five (5:2–6:10)
  - A. Second Nocturnal Search (5:2–8)
  - B. Christ Prefigured (5:9–16)
  - C. Christ Descends to His Garden (6:1–3)
  - D. Christ's Church Prefigured (6:4–10)

VI. Cycle Six
    A. The Shulammite and the Chariots (6:11–13)
    B. The Pleasures of Love (7:1–10)
    C. Paradise Restored (7:11–13)
    D. I Would Find You (8:1–4)
VII. Cycle Seven: Conclusion (8:5–14)
    A. Love: The Flame of Yah[weh] (8:5–7)
    B. Divine Love (8:8–12)
    C. Hasten, My Lover (8:13–14)

Introduction

Song of Solomon is the title given to an Old Testament book written by Solomon. Solomon was the son of David, Israel's greatest king, and the last monarch to rule over the united Hebrew Kingdom. Upon his death, the nation of Israel split into two kingdoms: the Northern Kingdom, known as Israel, and the Southern Kingdom, known as Judah. Viewed historically, Song of Solomon was written sometime during Solomon's forty-year reign, which scholars date about 961–922 BC.

You may recall that God appeared to Solomon in a dream, saying "Ask what I shall give you." In response, Solomon requested wisdom to govern God's people (1 Kings 3:5–9). We therefore see God's wisdom (demonstrated through Solomon) written in the pages of Song of Solomon, as well as in those of other books of wisdom literature authored by Solomon. Those other books, Proverbs and Ecclesiastes, are included in both the Jewish and Christian canons of Holy Scripture. Jewish tradition holds that Solomon composed Song of Solomon in his youth. As he grew older, he wrote Proverbs, and still later, when he became an old man and realized the vanity of things, he wrote Ecclesiastes.

As this study's title suggests, Song of Solomon epitomizes all the songs Solomon ever composed (the Bible teaches that Solomon composed 1,005 songs [1 Kings 4:32]). Among the Jewish people, Song of Solomon was read annually at Passover. This festival dovetails with the Song's celebration of Yahweh's love for Israel, a love which culminated in "marriage" during the Exodus. Modern-day Christians seldom hear the words of Song of Solomon read, for they seldom find their way into our lectionaries. However, we do occasionally find its themes weaving in and out of our hymns (e.g., "Jesus, the Very Thought of Thee" [*TLH* 350]).

With this insight, one could question why we should study Song of Solomon at all. The answer is a very simple one and deeply rooted in the Scriptures. Our Lord Jesus Christ implores us to search the Scriptures because "it is they that bear witness about me" (John 5:39). Throughout Song of Solomon, we repeatedly witness Christ's love for

His Church, a love which will culminate in the glorious “wedding” of His second coming. When we keep our study within the framework of God’s love for us in Christ, Song of Solomon becomes the most beautiful song ever written.

Lesson 1

Yearning for Love

Many scholars believe that Song of Solomon is one of three pieces of wisdom literature written by Solomon during his forty-year reign as Israel's king. In the Christian Bible, the book follows Proverbs and Ecclesiastes, two other books by the same author. Biblical scholars believe that the canonical order of Proverbs first, followed by Ecclesiastes and Song of Solomon, does not accurately depict the order in which they were written. They believe a more accurate order based on Solomon's maturity would place Song of Solomon first, followed by Proverbs and then Ecclesiastes.

Following Jewish tradition, some early Christian authors recommend that this book be read only after the age of thirty. Only then, when an individual was older and most likely married, could one fully understand and appreciate the nuptial imagery and sexual undertones found in this Song. At age thirty, an individual could approach this book without the snickering of adolescence and grasp the deeper meaning of a marriage blessed by God.

The theme of God's blessing of sex within the confines of marriage is reason enough to read Song of Solomon, but the message goes much deeper. Song of Solomon presents both Law and Gospel in a manner in which the Gospel predominates. In its pages we see God's love through Jesus Christ mirrored back to Him in the appropriate behavior of the baptized believer.

Setting the Stage

Although many commentaries on Song of Solomon already exist, including those of Martin Luther, most historians still consider it one of the Bible's most obscure books. In this study, we will examine Song of Solomon through the four stages of a maturing relationship. Stage one is anticipation: a longing, a desire for the relationship. Stage two brings the excitement of a couple's wedding. Stage three describes the blissful wedding consummation. Finally, stage four portrays the delightful, lasting marital relationship. As we examine these four stages, we must remember to view Song of Solomon as a testimony to our Lord Jesus Christ, who commanded us to search the Scriptures because they testify about Him (John 5:39).

1. Have you ever written a love song or a love poem? If you feel comfortable doing so, discuss the circumstances of its writing and how it impacted its intended recipient.

2. Do you remember the anticipation that accompanied a new relationship? Describe this anticipation in as much detail as you can recall.

Title and Authorship

As Song of Solomon begins, the author announces himself (1:1) and identifies this work as the epitome of songs. His superlative may bring to mind a television show of years past called "Your Show of Shows," thereby identifying this show as superior to all others. We identify Jesus Christ in much the same manner when we call Him the King of Kings and Lord of Lords. Solomon uses this superlative to let us know that, out of all the songs he has written, this is his magnum opus.

3. Most likely you are familiar with the source of Solomon's wisdom. Take a moment to refresh your memory by reading 1 Kings 3:3–9. From whom did Solomon seek wisdom and why?

4. 1 Kings 4:29–34 details the breadth of God's wisdom reflected in Solomon. Take a moment to discuss this wisdom.

5. Now scan the entire Song and note the number of references made to Solomon (e.g., 1:5), and the number of times he is called "king" (e.g., 1:3). How many did you find?

Anticipation

6. Read 1:2–4. The relational framework for this passage is that time between the wedding and the consummation of marriage. As yet, we do not know the identity of the actors in this love drama. The first speaker is only identified as "she" in our text. What does "she" desire?

7. We do not learn the identity of the "she" in this poem until 6:13. Scholars believe this is the same woman addressed in 1 Kings 1:1–4. Who is "she"?

8. The Christian Church longingly anticipates Christ's second coming just as "she" awaits her divine-human husband. Discuss this statement in light of John 14:2 and 1 John 3:2–3.

9. An ancient Jewish custom involved the anointing and perfuming of the bride in preparation for her wedding. Do you find anything in these verses which suggests the custom also applied to the

groom? If so, where? How might this perfuming relate to our heavenly Bridegroom, Jesus Christ, as found in John 12:3–7?

10. Verses 5–8 of our text harken back to a time early in the couple's romance. What do we learn about the Shulammite's physical appearance and her love for Solomon?

11. What did the Shulammite do that stirred her brothers to anger? How does the Shulammite's action show her love for Solomon?

12. Christ commands us to burn with passionate love for Him, just as the Shulammite burns with love for Solomon. Explain after reading Matthew 19:29.

God's Word for Today

13. As sinners, we stand before God and say, "Don't stare at me because I am stained with sin." Instead of treating us as our sins deserve, however, God sees us through the cross of Christ, and a great reversal occurs. Explain this great reversal as found in Romans 6:23.

14. It was common to refer to Israelite kings as shepherds. Shepherds tend sheep. What sheep did Solomon tend and who is the greatest shepherd (see Matthew 12:42 and John 10:11)?

In Closing

Encourage participants to begin the following activities:

- Consult a Bible dictionary for additional information on Abishag the Shulammite and Solomon.
- Learn more about Solomon's temple and magnificent palace. The account of their construction is recorded in 1 Kings 6:1–7:12.
- Read Solomon's psalms, Psalms 72 and 127.
- Read Song of Solomon 1:9–17 to prepare for the next session.

Close by singing or reading in unison the words of *Draw Us to Thee* (*LSB* 701; *LW* 153). As you do so, recall the Shulammite's request that Solomon *draw her* to him (1:3). As sinners, we pray that God's Holy Spirit would, through the Gospel, draw us ever closer to Him who died that we might live.

Draw us to Thee,
For then shall we
Walk in Thy steps forever
And hasten on
Where Thou art gone
To be with Thee, dear Savior.

Draw us to Thee,
Lord, lovingly;
Let us depart with gladness
That we may be
Forever free
From sorrow, grief, and sadness.

Draw us to Thee;
O grant that we
May walk the road to heaven!

Direct our way
Lest we should stray
And from Thy paths be driven.

Draw us to Thee
Unceasingly,
Into Thy kingdom take us;
Let us fore'er
Thy glory share,
Thy saints and joint heirs make us.

Lesson 2

The Bride Adorned

One of the most joyous occasions is at hand. The Shulammite prepares for her wedding. She asks others not to gaze at her because of her deeply-tanned skin (1:6). In contrast, the other women of Solomon's court purposely remained indoors to preserve a lighter complexion. Most likely, members of Solomon's court would have looked down their noses at the Shulammite, for her sun-kissed skin indicated she was not of the privileged royal caste. Her lowly background also meant she had nothing to offer Solomon; a marriage to this woman brought about no new national alliance or additional money for the royal coffers. In the Shulammite, we see the lowliness of our own estate. We have nothing of value to offer our Lord in return for His great love, only our pitiful selves. It is God's love through Jesus Christ that makes us as beautiful as the Shulammite whom Solomon calls the "most beautiful among women" (1:8).

Who is this Bride?

Some scholars suggest that the woman in this song is Abishag the Shulammite. Abishag was brought to King David in his old age (1 Kings 1:1–4) and, although she married David and he did lie in her arms, she remained a virgin (v. 4). Upon his death, David's son Adonijah asked to marry Abishag in a backdoor attempt to steal Solomon's claim to David's throne. When Solomon learned of this, he had his stepbrother put to death (1 Kings 2:13–26). A royal wedding would follow to solidify Solomon's power. As you read Song of Solomon, notice that the love Solomon has for the Shulammite, whether or not it is Abishag, is sincere. This is a wedding of love and not one of mere political convenience.

15. Discuss additional information on Solomon and Abishag found in your Bible dictionary.

16. If you are married or have been married, describe your personal preparations on your wedding day. If you are not married or have never been married, describe an event for which you spent a lot of time in personal preparation.

The Bride's Beauty

17. Read 1:9–11. These three verses show us the beauty of the Shulammite. As this scene unfolds, how does Solomon describe his future bride? How is this a compliment, considering all God did to the mighty Egyptian army (Exodus 14:26–28)?

18. The Shulammite has captured Solomon's heart. What other military images are used in the Song to describe her? Match the following verses with their imagery.

A. 6:4, 10 ______captivated Solomon

B. 8:10 ______bannered troops

C. 4:9 ______fortified city wall

19. Compare and discuss the Shulammite's description of herself in 1:6 with that of 1:9–11.

20. In ancient times, a woman's wedding preparations, especially when wedding a king, were an elaborate process that took an entire year. Explain the process, as found in Esther 2:12–13.

21. Notice the words of the chorus in verse 11 of our text. Here they promise to provide the bride with "ornaments of gold." After reading Genesis 24:52–53, explain the source of these gifts.

22. In Song of Solomon 1:12–17, the scene changes again from that of the wedding to that of the wedding consummation. Did you notice that Solomon called his wife "my love" in verse 15, a repeat of the same phrase used in verse 9? He uses this phrase again in 2:2, 10, 13; 4:1, 7; 5:2; and 6:4. A better translation is actually "my friend." Normally we would not consider the term *my friend* very endearing, but this term actually shows a special closeness. Explain this closeness as it relates to John 15:13–15.

23. What term of endearment does the Shulammite use when referring to Solomon in verses 1:13–14 and 2:3 and throughout the Song?

24. Nard grows in the Himalayan regions of India, is used in perfume making, and is very expensive. The aroma of nard (1:12) recalls another time when the aroma of nard filled a room. Read John 12:1–3 and explain the circumstances surrounding this outpouring of nard.

25. The symbolism continues with a reference to Solomon smelling myrrh. Myrrh is an aromatic gum found in southern Arabia. What is myrrh's tie to Jesus Christ (see Matthew 2:11; Mark 15:23; and John 19:39)?

26. Solomon's palace was so intricately built of cedar that it was called "the house of the forest of Lebanon." Read about its construction in 1 Kings 7:1–12 and describe its appearance.

27. How does Song of Solomon 1:12–17 indicate that the marriage was consummated in Solomon's palace?

God's Word for Today

28. Just as the groom showers his bride with gifts, Jesus Christ showers gifts on His bride, the Church (see Ephesians 5:26–27 and Galatians 3:27). Explain.

29. How does the Church respond to the wonderful gift of salvation (2 Corinthians 5:9)?

30. Read 1 Peter 1:18–19 and discuss the basis of Christ's gifts to the Church.

In Closing

Encourage participants to begin the following activities:

- Consult a Bible dictionary for information on roses and lilies.
- Define *adjuration*, a term we'll examine in our next lesson. Find its definition in your Bible dictionary or another dictionary.
- Read Song of Solomon 2:1–7 to prepare for the next session.

Close by singing or reading in unison the words of *How Sweet the Name of Jesus Sounds* (*LSB* 524; *LW* 279), recalling the military references of Song of Solomon 1:9 and the aromas emphasized in 1:12–17.

How sweet the name of Jesus sounds
  In a believer's ear!
It soothes our sorrows, heals our wounds,
  And drives away our fear.

It makes the wounded spirit whole
  And calms the heart's unrest;
'Tis manna to the hungry soul
  And to the weary, rest.

Dear name! The rock on which I build,
  My shield and hiding place;
My never-failing treasury filled
  With boundless stores of grace.

O Jesus, shepherd, guardian, friend,
  My Prophet, Priest, and King,
My Lord, my life, my way, my end,
  Accept the praise I bring.

How weak the effort of my heart,
How cold my warmest thought!
But when I see Thee as Thou art,
I'll praise Thee as I ought.

Till then I would Thy love proclaim
With ev'ry fleeting breath;
And may the music of Thy name
Refresh my soul in death!

Lesson 3

The Lily and the Apple Tree

Let us leave our newlyweds for a moment so that we might briefly trace the history of Song of Solomon. To date, the oldest manuscripts we have of the Song are four fragments discovered among the Dead Sea Scrolls. The discovery of these texts at Qumran further indicates the importance the ancient Hebrews placed on this book. This ascetic community at Qumran existed at the northern edge of the Dead Sea from about the second century BC to the first century AD, and their possession of the Song implies that this Jewish sect considered it to be canonical. Two out of the four textual fragments are shorter, leading scholars to conclude that these two scrolls were deliberately shortened, perhaps for liturgical use. Maybe the shorter text contained passages of devotional or liturgical favorites. Because Song of Solomon was in use at Qumran, a community known for its almost monastic existence, theologians conclude that it has a religious relevance that transcends its sexual undertones.

In the first millennium of the Christian era, Jewish scribes set about the task of offering textual notes on the Hebrew Old Testament, including Song of Solomon. Many of these "Masoretic texts" are well preserved and available for study. Amazingly, when the ancient Dead Sea Scrolls of Song of Solomon are laid beside those transcribed centuries later, we find very little variance between the two manuscripts. As with the entire biblical canon, God has faithfully preserved His Word that all might learn of Jesus Christ, the Word made flesh (John 1:14).

31. Look up *roses* and *lilies* in a Bible dictionary; discuss your findings.

32. If you feel comfortable, share a "pet name" you call your spouse, fiancé(e), or boy- or girlfriend.

Inside the Bridal Chamber

Our return to the bridal chamber finds Solomon and the Shulammite alone together on their wedding night. As chapter 2 begins, she speaks about herself.

33. Read 2:1–2. To what does the Shulammite compare herself in these verses?

34. Flowers play a recurring role throughout Song of Solomon. The "rose" of Sharon mentioned in verse one has its origins in the King James translation of the Bible (AD 1611). Although scholars debate about the exact identity of this flower, some believe that the "rose" is an asphodel, a common white, yellow, or even pink flower of the lily family indigenous to the area known as Sharon. What would the Shulammite mean when she refers to herself as an asphodel? How do her words match the meaning of 1:5–6?

35. How does Solomon respond to his wife's self-effacing comments that she is no more than a common lily? How do his words fit Paul's exhortation in Ephesians 5:25, 28–29?

36. Theologically, we have compared the Shulammite to the Christian Church. How might we rightly call the Church "a lily among brambles"?

In Love's Embrace

37. Read 2:3–6. To what fruit tree is Solomon compared? In our theological references, we noted that Solomon is to Christ as the Shulammite is to the Church. How might Jesus Christ compare to a fruit tree whose sap sustains His Church (see John 15:5 as you develop your answer)?

38. Examine the passionate wording of 2:3. In what does the Shulammite delight? Can you relate to her feeling about being so close to the one you love? Explain. Since the Shulammite corresponds to the Christian Church and Solomon to Jesus Christ, what theological statement is made in this verse?

39. Where might the Church find sustenance to survive as "lilies among the brambles"? Matthew records the answer in his Gospel (26:26–28).

The Adjuration

40. Read 2:7. How does your Bible dictionary or other dictionary define the word *adjuration*? Wisdom literature, of which Song of

Solomon is part, often draws upon creation to teach the wisdom of the Creator. To whom does the Shulammite appeal?

41. What estate is ordained by God for the enjoyment and pleasure of physical love (see Genesis 2:24 and Matthew 19:5–6)? What warning does Paul give in 1 Corinthians 6:16–18? In light of these three passages, discuss the content of the Shulammite's adjuration.

42. Does this adjuration apply to women only? Why or why not?

43. None of the consequences of "arousing the love until it pleases [God]" are spoken about in this Song. What are some of the consequences? Take time also to discuss problems in society that also result from "arousing love" prematurely. How might members of God's family help one another prevent this?

God's Word for Today

44. Paul characterizes love in 1 Corinthians 13:4–7. Take a moment to read this passage. Jesus Christ personifies these words (John 15:13). How might we, as twenty-first-century sinners, receive forgiveness and enjoy a personal relationship with the font of all love (see 1 Corinthians 11:23–26)?

45. Perhaps you know someone who has "awakened love" prematurely; God does not desire eternal punishment for them. Read Ezekiel 18:23, 32; 33:11 and explain God's loving and merciful desire for all sinners.

In Closing

Encourage participants to begin the following activities:

- If you are or have been married, be prepared to discuss the anticipation and planning that led up to your engagement.
- Think about this question: At what time of year might the earth most closely resemble the Garden of Eden?
- Read Song of Solomon 2:8–17 to prepare for the next session.

Close by singing or reading in unison the words of *Come Down, O Love Divine* (*LSB* 501; *LW* 162), noticing how love is personified in this hymn.

Come down, O Love divine;
Seek Thou this soul of mine,
And visit it with Thine own ardor glowing;
O Comforter, draw near;
Within my heart appear,
And kindle it, Thy holy flame bestowing.

O let it freely burn,
Till worldly passions turn
To dust and ashes in its heat consuming;
And let Thy glorious light
Shine ever on my sight,
And clothe me round, the while my path illuming.

Let holy charity
Mine outward vesture be
And lowliness become mine inner clothing—
True lowliness of heart,
Which takes the humbler part,
And o'er its own shortcomings weeps with loathing.

And so the yearning strong,
With which the soul will long,
Shall far outpass the pow'r of human telling;
No soul can guess His grace
Till it become the place
Wherein the Holy Spirit makes His dwelling.

Lesson 4

A Spring Marriage Proposal

Married couples remember the major events in their relationship such as first dates, special dates, who they were with when they first met, and their first kiss. Most can recall with vivid detail the day they became engaged. Men may recall the days leading up to the events, such as searching for just the right ring and orchestrating events so they reach a crescendo with the question, "Will you marry me?" Women may recall the "butterflies" of anticipation and wondering, Is this the day?

For Solomon and the Shulammite, the day has arrived. Their engagement is at hand. In ancient times, engagements were often arranged through negotiations between families or, in the case of a prince or king, through an emissary. In many instances, couples met for the first time as the wedding ceremony commenced. Not so in the case of Solomon and the Shulammite, as we are about to witness. Their engagement unfolds much like an engagement in the twenty-first century. For them, an engagement to marry is a natural outgrowth of the love God has planted and nurtured within them (8:6).

The location of the Shulammite changes as Solomon's Song moves into 2:8. The couple is no longer found in love's embrace on their wedding night. Instead, the Shulammite flashes back to a time of anticipation; perhaps she and Solomon have already spoken words of affection for one another. Now she has returned home to her mother (6:9) and brothers (1:6). Dreamily, she gazes out a window and sees her beloved in the distance. Her heart races as she wonders whether this is the day.

Anticipation

46. If you are married or have been married, recall in as much detail as possible the events leading up to your engagement. If you are

single, recall the anticipation of asking someone for a date or waiting for a certain someone to call.

47. According to Revelation 21:1–4, for what event does the universal Church wait in anticipation?

48. Read Song of Solomon 2:8–10. The Shulammite peers into the distance and sees Solomon. Discuss the simile she uses to describe him. What might such a comparison symbolize?

Courtship

49. What words in verses 8–10 indicate that we are viewing the couple's lives during a period of courtship, rather than a period of married life? In your mind, do the words found here paint a picture of romance? Describe it. What makes this courtship so unique?

50. Read Solomon's words in 2:10–14. What words comprise Solomon's marriage proposal? (Hint: They are spoken twice in our text.)

51. In His great wisdom, God continually calls us to faith just as Solomon called the Shulammite to be his bride. Witness how God calls Israel to faith in Isaiah 52:1 and 60:1. Since Jesus Christ has come, we

anticipate His second coming. What words of admonition do we find in Matthew 25:1–13?

52. Can you determine from our reading the time of year in which Solomon proposes to the Shulammite? Keep in mind that the rainy season in Israel lasts from October through April.

53. Some scholars marvel at the way this section of the Song is written. It seems to heighten the reader's senses as it recalls the return of spring. Blossoms perfume the air and the turtledoves call (2:12). In a fleeting moment, we glimpse the Garden of Eden. These words parallel 4:1–11, where God's creative hand is seen throughout nature. Yet the Lord has even greater things in store for those who believe on His name. What are these? Explain what you find in Isaiah 42:5–9.

54. Read 2:15. Ancient literature attests to foxes digging up grape vines and eating the young fruit. Symbolically, grapevines represent a much larger motif in both the Old and New Testaments. What do they represent according to Isaiah 5:1–7 and Matthew 20:1–16? Who are the foxes according to Ezekiel 13:4? (Note: The word *jackals* appears in some translations instead of *foxes*, but the meaning remains the same.)

55. Read Song of Solomon 2:16–20. One of the most beautiful passages of the Song appears in verse 16. Statements saying that the man became the wife's husband and that the husband belongs to the wife are extremely rare in Old Testament marriage descriptions. To this day, some Jewish couples have 2:16 engraved on the inside of their

wedding bands. Compare Song of Solomon 2:16 to 1 Corinthians 7:3–5. Are they saying the same thing? Why or why not?

God's Word for Today

56. Read Ephesians 5:21–33. How might the covenant of marriage in a small way be a copy of God's covenant with His people?

57. In Song of Solomon 2:17, we read of "shadows flee[ing]" as night approaches. Sin casts darkness over our lives in the same manner, but, through His Son, God has done a marvelous deed. The apostle Peter explains what this marvelous deed is in 2 Peter 1:19. What is it?

In Closing

Encourage participants to begin the following activities:

- Recall a time when you were apart from the one you love and did not know the exact whereabouts of the other.
- In our next lesson, we will discuss the search motif of Song of Solomon. How might searching relate to God? to you and me?
- Read Song of Solomon 3:1–5 to prepare for the next session.

Close by singing or reading in unison the words of *The Bridegroom Soon Will Call Us* (*LW* 176).

The Bridegroom soon will call us,
"Come to the wedding feast."
May slumber not befall us
Nor watchfulness decrease.
But may our lamps be burning

With oil enough and more
That, with our Lord returning,
We find an open door.

Then, oh, what jubilation
To see our Savior's face,
His glorious exaltation
Since winning us God's grace.
Then kings will come to meet us
And psalmists rich in song,
Apostles, prophets greet us,
A great and splendid throng.

The Christ, his glory sharing,
Will give us crowns of gold
He won for us by wearing
Thorned agonies untold.
The Father with embraces
Will welcome us, each one,
Robed in the Spirit's graces
As princely as God's Son.

Like skies in joyous motion
Or music after tears,
New song will fill the ocean
Of heaven's ageless years
While angel hosts are raising
With saints from great to least
The anthem tides for praising
The Giver of this feast.

Prayer: Merciful Lord, Thank You for calling us to eternal life through faith in Your Son. By Your grace the great wedding feast is ours. Thank You, Lord. Amen.

Lesson 5

The First Nocturnal Search

The third of six cycles in the Song of Solomon begins with 3:1 and ends with 4:7. Like the previous two cycles, this cycle is divided into three sections, with the first five verses completing a section on courtship. This is followed by a wedding procession of six verses and a wedding/consummation section of seven verses. In addition, the first of two dramatic late-night searches by the Shulammite starts this section and we find a portrait of the Shulammite as Solomon's bride. She is dressed, perfumed, veiled, and carried on a litter to her wedding. We learn of her flawless beauty as seen through Solomon's eyes.

The two most dramatic illustrations of the search theme found in the Song are 3:1–5 and 5:2–8. In both sections, the Shulammite searches through the streets of Jerusalem for Solomon. Drawing again on our parallels of the Shulammite representing the Church and Solomon representing our Savior, Jesus Christ, it is easy to conclude that those loved by Jesus would seek Him where He has promised to be found: in His Word and Sacraments. Similarly, we might draw a comparison between the Shulammite's search and Mary Magdalene's search for Jesus that first Easter morning (John 20:1–2, 11). We may favorably compare the emotions expressed by the women at the tomb with those expressed during the Shulammite's search: the emotions of fear, trepidation, and haste.

Lost Love

58. Recall a time when you were apart from the one you love and did not know his or her whereabouts.

59. Describe the emotional feelings you experienced during your search and the relief you felt when at last you were reunited.

The Shulammite's First Nocturnal Search

60. Read 3:1–4. Scholars believe that, while the Shulammite was employed in the service of King David, her mother was provided a home in Jerusalem where she stayed. This home in the city allowed her to be near her daughter. As our third cycle begins, the Shulammite is betrothed to Solomon but living in her mother's home. How can scholars conclude that the Shulammite is only betrothed and not married to Solomon? Examine the evidence for yourself. Contrast the pronouns found in 3:1 with those of 1:12, 16–17 and explain what you find.

61. Unlike the Greek language, which boasts of a variety of ways to express the word *love,* the most common Hebrew word for *love* is very limited and indicates an ongoing emotion. We see it expressed in the words of the virgins in 1:3–4. For the Shulammite, her love for Solomon is even deeper. Hers is a love that God has ignited (8:6–7). What words does she choose to express her love for Solomon? Perhaps you have noticed that she uses these words on four occasions within our text.

62. In the eighth century AD, the Venerable Bede noticed a similarity between the Shulammite's search for Solomon and Mary Magdalene's search for Jesus. Read about Mary Magdalene's search in John 20:1, 11–18 and compare it with the words of Song of Solomon 3:1–5. How many areas of similarity do you find?

Faithful Helpers

63. When does the Shulammite begin her search for Solomon (v. 1) and whom does she enlist to aid her search (v. 3)?

64. In Old Testament times, watchmen were strategically placed throughout the city to guard it from attack. Some watchmen lined the city walls while others patrolled the streets. In 3:1–4, the Shulammite encounters helpful watchmen, but later in 5:7 we see a different picture altogether. Stepping back to view this portion of the Song theologically, who might the helpful watchmen be, according to Ezekiel 3:17 and Isaiah 62:6–9?

65. Who are our spiritual watchmen today? Read 2 Corinthians 5:20. What important function do these spiritual watchmen perform?

66. Although the Shulammite and Solomon are not yet married, this flashback shows her obvious delight in finding "him whom my soul loves." What words in Song of Solomon 3:4 show the Shulammite's anticipation of her wedding day and the consummation to follow?

A Second Adjuration

67. Song of Solomon 3:5 closes with an adjuration identical to the one in 2:7 (a third and much shorter adjuration is located in 5:8 and a fourth in 8:4). How might this adjuration signal that it is the Shulammite's love for Solomon that drove her late at night into the

streets of Jerusalem in search of him, and that this love is so powerful that it should not be aroused prematurely?

God's Word for Today

68. When the Bible repeats a point several times, as it does in the case of the adjurations, it means that it is important to note and remember. What point is God making and why is it so important in a society that savors instant gratification? What does God offer to those who have already aroused love prematurely (Romans 10:9)?

69. Sin separates us from God. As the Holy Spirit works faith in us, He compels us to search for Jesus Christ, the One "greater than Solomon" (Matthew 12:42). Where can we find "Him whom my soul loves" (Song of Solomon 3:4; see Matthew 28:18–20; 1 Corinthians 10:16–17; and Philippians 2:16)?

In Closing

Encourage participants to begin the following activities:

- Describe in as much detail as possible how you dressed on your wedding day. For singles, describe how you dressed for an important event.
- How did you travel on your wedding day? by car? by limousine?
- Read Song of Solomon 3:6–11 to prepare for the next session.

Close by singing or reciting together the words of *Jesus, Lover of My Soul* (*LW* 508:1, 2, 4).

Jesus, lover of my soul,
Let me to Thy mercy fly
While the nearer waters roll,
While the tempest still is high.
Hide me, O my Savior, hide
Till the storm of life is past;
Safe into the haven guide.
Oh, receive my soul at last.

Other refuge have I none;
Hangs my helpless soul on thee.
Leave, ah, leave me not alone,
Still support and comfort me!
All my trust on Thee is stayed,
All my help from Thee I bring,
Cover my defenseless head
With the shadow of Thy wing.

Thou, O Christ, art all I want;
More than all in thee I find.
Raise the fallen, cheer the faint,
Heal the sick, and lead the blind.
Just and holy is thy name;
I am all unrighteousness,
False and full of sin I am;
Thou art full of truth and grace.

Lesson 6

The Wedding Day

Attend most Christian weddings and chances are you will find many features in common. Usually, the groom and groomsmen enter from the front of the sanctuary to await the entry of the bride and her bridesmaids. As the music begins, all eyes shift from the groom fidgeting in his tuxedo to the beautifully adorned bridesmaids and the bride, who has never looked lovelier. The months of planning all come down to this single moment when she makes her grand entrance. Dressed in a white or ivory gown, she enters to the honor of all those in attendance. On her head the bride wears a veil, which may flow down her back. Her personal attendant adjusts the train of her dress as traditional music plays. Then the bride, normally escorted by her father, processes to the altar for the wedding ceremony, which includes vows recited in the presence of Almighty God.

Wedding processions are not new. In fact, we are about to witness the wedding procession of Solomon and the Shulammite, a procession that took place nearly three thousand years ago. The words that appear in 3:1–11 provide part two of the third cycle of Song of Solomon. Included in our text is a description of a wedding procession so detailed that we may feel as if we were among the throng in attendance that day. This beautiful procession, just like countless others today, ends in a wedding ceremony before God. Let us go back in time.

Your Wedding Remembered

70. Describe in as much detail as possible how you dressed for your wedding day. For singles, describe how you dressed for an important occasion, such as a wedding. Do you remember the ceremony itself?

71. If you are married or have been married, recall how you traveled on your wedding day. Was it by car? by limousine?

The Wedding Procession and the Exodus

72. The wedding of Solomon and the Shulammite is found in 3:6–11. Read it aloud. The narrator of this section of Scripture is the chorus identified only as "they" in some translations. In keeping with the remainder of the Song, this chorus is identified as the "daughters of Jerusalem" to whom the adjurations of 2:7 and 3:5 are addressed. They are also the likely speakers in 1:4; 5:9; 6:1; and 8:5. The arrival of the Shulammite for her royal wedding (3:6) recalls the days of the exodus. After reading Exodus 13:21–22, compare these two events.

73. For centuries, the traditional Jewish interpretation of Song of Solomon compared Solomon's marriage to the Shulammite with God's marriage to the Israelites during the Exodus. This spiritual wedding is supported by Jeremiah 2:2; Hosea 2:14–16; and Ezekiel 16. Explain.

74. In the New Testament, the image of God's marriage to His people (Christ to the Church) culminates in a great wedding feast. Read and discuss how Matthew 22:1–14; 1 Corinthians 6:19–20; Revelation 5:9; Ephesians 5:22–23; and Revelation 19:6–10 support such a view.

75. Take a few minutes to describe the procession of the Shulammite. How does she arrive? To whom does her transportation belong? Who accompanies her on her journey?

76. Describe Solomon's arrival (3:9–10). Solomon's carriage brings to mind images of Solomon's temple and his home. What are the similarities you find as you read 1 Kings 7:2–3, 28, 30; and 2 Chronicles 2:6, 14?

77. Can you visualize the contrast between the procession of the Shulammite and that of Solomon? Now compare the nation of Israel (the Shulammite) and God (represented by Solomon).

78. The wedding ceremony of Song of Solomon 3:11 is portrayed much like a coronation event in which Solomon's reign is established in a new way. How does the custom of wearing crowns match up with the words of Revelation 4:4, 10 and 3:11 thanks to the sacrificial death of Jesus Christ?

The Wedding Night

79. Solomon speaks the words of 4:1–7 on his wedding night. They are a complimentary portrait of his bride. Read them aloud. To what does he compare her eyes? In Old Testament times, the sheep of Syria and Palestine were white, but the goats were black. With that information in hand, what color was the Shulammite's hair?

80. You may recall the Shulammite's two adjurations, which we studied previously. Now that the couple is married (3:11), Solomon pronounces his intent to go "to the mountain of myrrh and the hill of frankincense" (4:6) to consummate the marriage. What does this order of events teach about the premature arousal of love "until it pleases" (2:7; 3:5)?

God's Word for Today

81. The words of Ephesians 5:21–33 are often read at weddings. Here, Paul expresses the details of a God-pleasing marriage. Discuss what a God-pleasing marriage looks like and how it is analogous to Christ and the Church.

82. Solomon expresses his complete satisfaction with his new bride in Song of Solomon 4:7. She is flawless. Compare Solomon's satisfaction to the words of Ephesians 5:26–27. What makes believers holy and blameless before God?

In Closing

Encourage participants to begin the following activities:

- Read the account of the Garden of Eden found in Genesis 2:4–25.
- What was the relationship like between God and man? between man and wife in God's garden?
- Read Song of Solomon 4:1–7 to prepare for the next session.

Close by singing or saying in unison the words of *The Church's One Foundation* (*LSB* 644:1, 2, 5; *LW* 289:1, 2, 6).

The Church's one foundation
   Is Jesus Christ, her Lord;
She is His new creation
   By water and the Word.
From heav'n He came and sought her
   To be His holy bride;
With His own blood He bought her,
   And for her life He died.

Elect from ev'ry nation,
   Yet one o'er all the earth;
Her charter of salvation:
   One Lord, one faith, one birth.
One holy name she blesses,
   Partakes one holy food,
And to one hope she presses
   With ev'ry grace endued.

Yet she on earth has union
   With God, the Three in One,
And mystic sweet communion
   With those whose rest is won.
O blessèd heav'nly chorus!
   Lord, save us by Your grace
That we, like saints before us,
   May see You face to face.

Lesson 7

Visions of Eden

This section of our study marks a transition. In it, we find the culmination of the fourth cycle of Song of Solomon. So far, we have primarily examined the relationship of Solomon and the Shulammite through their courtship and their wedding. All of the remaining cycles will explore the continuing love affair after their marriage. In this session, we will witness again the three stages of relational development found in earlier sessions; however, this is the last time we will review the stages of courtship, wedding, and consummation.

God ordained the perfect relationship between man and wife in the Garden of Eden. After God had finished creating heaven and earth and filling it with all manner of living things, He created humans, the epitome of His work of creation. On the sixth day of creation, God created Adam from the dust of the earth and gave him a soul. God drew Eve from Adam's side to serve as his helper (Genesis 2:20), leading to God's pronouncement that His creation "was very good" (Genesis 1:31). We cannot comprehend the beauty of God's creation before sin entered the world. Its beauty surpasses our feeble understanding. The love between God and humankind and between man and wife was unmatched before sin ruined everything. While God's good creation remains, its perfection is gone and with it the once perfect relationship between husband and wife. However, while we are left with only fleeting glimpses of the old Eden, we eagerly await the new Eden of an eternity with God made possible by the blood of Jesus Christ. In Song of Solomon 4:8–5:1, we find a fleeting glimpse of the earliest days of creation and a glimpse forward into life eternal.

The Garden of Eden—Your Perspective

83. At the close of our previous session you were asked to read about the Garden of Eden (Genesis 2:4–25). Read and discuss that passage now.

84. Contrast the differences in relationships between God and humankind and between husband and wife then and now.

Another View of Solomon's Proposal

85. Read 4:8. One can almost imagine the location described here (see 2:8–10). Where might Solomon have spoken these words and when?

86. Mount Hermon is one of several peaks in the Anti-Lebanon. If the Shulammite stood on the summit of Mount Hermon and looked south, she would have seen a good deal of the land God promised to the ancient Israelites. Through poetic verse, what is Solomon's invitation?

At the Altar

87. Now read 4:9–15. A widely accepted scholarly view claims that these words are spoken by Solomon (all but those spoken by the "others" at the end of 5:1) as the Shulammite stands before him during the wedding ceremony. How does this passage confirm that the couple is now married (4:9–12; 5:1)? How does the word *bride* in our text support the understanding that this wedding symbolizes God's union with His Church (Isaiah 62:1–5)?

88. Solomon's wordplay describing his wife's kisses is very romantic. How does he describe them (v. 11)? Explain how Solomon's words harken back to the time of the exodus (see Exodus 3:8, 17; Joshua 5:6).

89. What other terms of endearment does Solomon use throughout Song 4:8–5:1?

The Locked Garden

90. In 4:12–15, Solomon refers to his new wife as "a garden locked," "a spring locked," and "a fountain sealed" (the mention of spices and fragrances indicate the presence of God in this union). From what we have already learned about the Shulammite, how do these terms aptly describe her? The Hebrew word meaning "sealed up" also applies to those whose sins are forgiven by God's abundant grace. How is *sealed* used in Ephesians 1:13–14?

91. God sealed up another garden unsurpassed in beauty and fragrances and beyond imagining. What was it (Genesis 3:23–24)? In the ancient Near East, kings often had a garden paradise signifying their desire that God would bless this king's land as He once did ages before (Genesis 2:10–12). According to Christ's gracious promise, when will believers enjoy paradise (Revelation 2:7)?

92. Solomon toasts his wife's beauty by referring to her as "a well of living water" (4:15). Jesus uses similar words in His encounter with

the Samaritan woman (John 4:10–14). Explain what Jesus means when He speaks about "living water."

93. Verses 4:16–5:1 complete this session. Read them aloud. This completes the stages common among the cycles of the first half of Song of Solomon: courtship, marriage, and consummation. God has blessed marriage with a mutual belonging between husband and wife. In this case, the Shulammite invites Solomon to enjoy "his garden" (v. 16b). How do her words dovetail with those of 1 Corinthians 7:4?

94. The friends of the bride and groom complete this section of Scripture (5:1). What do they encourage the married couple to do?

God's Word for Today

95. As sinners, we deserve nothing less than eternal separation from God (Romans 6:23a). Instead, Christ offers us salvation as "living water." Apply this to Acts 2:38–39 and Ephesians 5:26–27.

In Closing

Encourage participants to begin the following activities:

- Reread the Shulammite's first nocturnal search in 3:1–5.
- Recall times when your relationship with another was on rocky ground.

- Read 5:2–8 to prepare for the next session.

Close by singing or saying together the words of *Beautiful Savior* (*LSB* 537; *LW* 507).

Beautiful Savior,
King of creation,
Son of God and Son of Man!
Truly I'd love Thee,
Truly I'd serve Thee,
Light of my soul, my joy, my crown.

Fair are the meadows,
Fair are the woodlands,
Robed in flow'rs of blooming spring;
Jesus is fairer,
Jesus is purer,
He makes our sorr'wing spirit sing.

Fair is the sunshine,
Fair is the moonlight,
Bright the sparkling stars on high;
Jesus shines brighter,
Jesus shines purer
Than all the angels in the sky.

Beautiful Savior,
Lord of the nations,
Son of God and Son of Man!
Glory and honor,
Praise, adoration
Now and forevermore be Thine!

Pray: Lord, you richly bless us through relationships, whether those of marriage or through friendships with fellow believers. Strengthen our faith, that we may know the lasting joy of eternal life with You. We pray in Jesus' name. Amen.

Lesson 8

Second Nocturnal Search

Song of Solomon 5:2–8 marks the halfway point of this historic view of marriage recorded by King Solomon. No longer will each cycle contain the three characteristics of courtship, wedding, and consummation found earlier. Instead, we will glimpse the relationship between Solomon and the Shulammite at strategic times during their ongoing marriage.

Marital relationships change as time passes. All too soon, the anticipation and yearning for each other gives way to child-rearing, (although that dynamic is not mentioned in the case of Solomon and the Shulammite), homemaking, career building, hobbies, sports, and friends. As couples move from phase to phase, marriages may buckle under the strain. Sometimes the strain is too great and separation, even divorce, results. Since the fall of humankind, marriages only resemble in part what God intended. Now they are but a poor reflection. To unfold God's original plan for marriage, we need only read Ephesians 5:21–33. Because of sin, storms in marriage are as inevitable as day following night. "For just as there are changes of weather, so war follows peace, happiness follows sorrow, consolation follows affliction—and then some new affliction follows consolation . . . This is the way it must always be in this kingdom" (Martin Luther).

For Solomon and his new bride changes are coming: the passing of time sees to that. Song of Solomon provides no interlude, no look at intervening events. Instead, it transitions smoothly to a view of the same couple years later. Notice the changes.

Changes and Conflict

96. At the end of our last lesson, you were asked to recall a time when a relationship you knew about was on rocky ground. If you feel comfortable, share that experience with the group.

97. How was the conflict resolved?

The Dream

Read Song of Solomon 5:2–8.

98. A noted Bible commentator divides these eight verses into two parts. The first four verses comprise the first part, while the remaining three verses comprise the second. Verse five serves as a transition verse between the two. This Old Testament scholar contends that the first four verses are part of the Shulammite's dream while the other three verses are reality. What words in verse 2 substantiate the belief that the Shulammite is dreaming?

99. Compare 3:1 to 5:2. What difference do you find in the way the Shulammite refers to Solomon? This difference allows scholars to conclude that, beginning with 5:2, we are looking at a period of time after the couple's wedding.

100. What words of endearment does Solomon use in 4:8–12 (omitted in 5:2) that indicate we are viewing them in a later stage of their marriage?

101. We can almost picture Solomon calling to his bride through a latticed window (5:2, 4). In her dream, why does the Shulammite deny Solomon access to her bedchamber? This encounter between

Solomon and the Shulammite is similar to the parable Jesus teaches in Luke 11:5–8. Explain.

Reality and the Search

102. Her dream is so real that the Shulammite rises to let Solomon in, but what is the reality (Song of Solomon 5:6)?

103. The Shulammite's search for Solomon has a New Testament parallel in the experience of Mary at the tomb (Mark 16:1–8). Describe the emotions each of these women felt.

104. Theologically, Solomon represents Jesus Christ and the Shulammite represents the Church. How do the Shulammite's words in Song of Solomon 5:6 correspond to those of Isaiah 65:12? God made a promise to all those who seek him (Isaiah 65:1). What is that promise and what assurance does it give?

105. The actions of the watchmen in 5:7 stand in shocking contrast to those in 3:3–4. Discuss the different reactions.

106. Scholars see the watchmen as representing the office of the pastoral ministry. Ancient watchmen (like pastors) are charged with the responsibility of guarding the virtue of those within the city walls and not just their general well-being. Based on Ezekiel 23:28–30, we

might rightfully conclude that the chastising of the Shulammite by the watchmen was a case of mistaken identity. How so?

Another Adjuration

107. To whom is the adjuration of 5:8 addressed? What are they sworn to do? To whom does this adjuration ultimately appeal?

God's Word for Today

108. The Christian Church suffers greatly for her faith in following Jesus Christ. We read daily about the persecution of Christ's Church throughout the world. Relate Ephesians 4:8; John 16:7; and John 16:16 to the Church as prefigured in the person of the Shulammite.

109. The Shulammite's adjuration is similar to Jesus teaching about the cost of discipleship (see Matthew 8:18–22; 10:34–39; and Luke 14:28–33). What wonderful Gospel promise is given to baptized believers who suffer for Christ's sake (Romans 5:3–5; 6:3–7)?

In Closing

Encourage participants to begin the following activities:

- How would you describe your husband/wife/boyfriend/girlfriend?
- Be prepared to discuss this statement: A spiritual war exists between those who believe in the salvation offered through Jesus Christ alone and those who do not.
- Read Song of Solomon 5:9–6:10 to prepare for the next session.

Speak or sing together the words of *Seek Where You May to Find a Way* (*LSB* 557; *LW* 358).

Seek where you may
To find a way
    That leads to your salvation.
My heart is stilled,
On Christ I build,
    He is the one foundation.
His Word is sure,
His works endure;
    He overthrows
    All evil foes;
Through Him I more than conquer.

Seek whom you may
To be your stay,
    None can redeem his brother.
All helpers failed;
This man prevailed,
    The God-man and none other,
Our Servant-King
Of whom we sing.
    We're justified
    Because He died,
The guilty being guiltless.

Seek Him alone
Who did atone,
    Who did your souls deliver.
O seek Him first,
All you who thirst

For grace that fails you never.
In ev'ry need
Seek Him indeed;
To ev'ry heart
He will impart
His blessings without measure.

My heart's delight,
My crown most bright,
O Christ, my joy forever.
Not wealth nor pride
Nor fortune's tide
Our bonds of love shall sever.
You are my Lord;
Your precious Word
Shall guide my way
And help me stay
Forever in Your presence.

Prayer: Precious Savior, You came to redeem us to Yourself. Your Holy Spirit seeks us in our despair and through Your Gospel works to strengthen our faith. Save us, we pray, in Your Holy name. Amen.

Lesson 9

Christ and His Church Prefigured

The Shulammite is sick with love (5:8). Her love has caused her to dream about Solomon when he is not near her side. Her dream seems so real, she rises in search of Solomon. She wanders the streets of Jerusalem, where the city's watchmen not only guard the city from invaders, but also guard the city's moral character. These watchmen mistake the Shulammite for a harlot; they chastise her and strike her (5:7). In accordance with Jewish law, these same watchmen remove the Shulammite's veil, exposing her to public ridicule (v. 7).

Certainly, a parallel exists between the Shulammite and the persecuted Christian Church. This parallel extends beyond the lighted human torches and the colosseum slaughter of ancient Rome; twenty centuries later in places like the Sudan, mass genocide of Christians occurs with a frequency rivaling the atrocities of the most hideous of emperors. In the United States, prayers are forbidden in public schools and epithets of "intolerance" are hurled at those who prescribe a traditional morality. Meanwhile, Satan, the great incrementalist, tears at the fabric of society, satisfied to remove one fiber at a time, over centuries, if he must.

In her late-night search, the Shulammite is temporarily thwarted from achieving her goal. So, too, the Church. An unsuccessful initial search does not end the dream of a love reunited. For the Shulammite, joy is near. For Christians, the wait continues a bit longer, until our joy is made complete—when Christ comes again in all His glory. We are about to preview this glory in a spectacular word picture found in Song of Solomon.

Digging a Little Deeper

110. At the end of our last session, you were asked how you would describe your husband/wife/boyfriend/girlfriend. Take a moment to do that now.

Christ Prefigured in Solomon

When we last saw the Shulammite, she was delivering an adjuration to the daughters of Jerusalem. She charged them to find Solomon because she was "sick with love" (5:8). What follows over the next few verses (5:9–6:10) is the most detailed recounting of Solomon's features. This is followed by those of the Shulammite. In themselves, these portray Christ and His Church prefigured in human form.

111. After reading 5:9, discuss how the daughters of Jerusalem respond to the Shulammite's adjuration.

112. While intimate portraits of the Shulammite are found throughout Song of Solomon (i.e., 4:1–5), until now we have had no intimate portrait of Solomon. How does the Shulammite describe Solomon in a way that will enable the daughters of Jerusalem to begin their search (5:10–16)?

113. Are there words in 5:10–16 that conjure up images of a king? a priest? the Garden of Eden? What are they, and where are they found?

114. Years after the events described in 5:10–16, Ezekiel, Daniel, and the Synoptic Gospels (Matthew, Mark, and Luke) recorded similar images. How are the images found in Ezekiel 1:25–29; Daniel 2:31–35; Matthew 17:1–3; Mark 9:2–4; and Luke 9:28–29 similar to those in Song of Solomon 5:10–16?

115. The reign of Solomon ushered in the wealthiest era in the history of the Israelites. What precious metals and priceless gems does the Shulammite use to describe Solomon? These valuable jewels carry a special significance because they recall the past and project the future. Explain this statement in light of Exodus 39:8–14 and Revelation 21:19–21.

116. Although the jewels mentioned in the Shulammite's description of Solomon are extremely valuable, baptized believers were ransomed from sin with something far more valuable. What did Jesus offer in exchange for our lives (1 Peter 1:18–19)? On what precious stone is our faith built (1 Peter 2:4–8)?

Solomon's Location

117. Begin this section of our study by reading Song of Solomon 6:1–3. Now that the daughters of Jerusalem are equipped with Solomon's description, what is their next question? What commands are they keeping by their actions (Exodus 20:14, 17)?

118. Scripture does not record how the Shulammite became aware of Solomon's location, but she reveals his location to the

daughters of Jerusalem (6:2). The Shulammite's love for Solomon is maturing. Make the correlation between her words in 6:3 and those of 2:16. Her full maturity in their marital relationship is found in 7:10. Explain. What does selflessness mean to a marriage? Cite specific examples.

The Shulammite: Christ's Church Prefigured

119. Read 6:4–10. Upon their reunification, Solomon recalls his earlier description of the Shulammite (6:5c–7; 4:1–3). With what words does he call her unique among women?

120. In 6:10, Solomon depicts his wife in a theological manner. How so? Where does the Church receive her righteousness to shine "bright as the sun" (Galatians 3:27)?

God's Word for Today

121. The Shulammite is "bannered" (6:10). Her love, with God as its origin, has conquered Solomon's heart. Commentators through the ages also see here a great reversal. She who had nothing now shines with great brilliance. Colossians 1:15–20 teaches that Christians benefit from an even greater reversal. Discuss this reversal.

In Closing

Encourage participants to begin the following activities:

- Comment on Martin Luther's thought that we should recognize God's gifts in other people.
- Read Song of Solomon 6:11–8:4 to prepare for the next session.

Speak or sing together the words of *Stand Up, Stand Up for Jesus* (*LSB* 660; *LW* 305).

Stand up, stand up for Jesus,
  Ye soldiers of the cross.
Lift high His royal banner;
  It must not suffer loss.
From vict'ry unto vict'ry
  His army He shall lead
Till ev'ry foe is vanquished,
  And Christ is Lord indeed.

Stand up, stand up for Jesus;
  The trumpet call obey;
Stand forth in mighty conflict
  In this His glorious day.
Let all His faithful serve Him
  Against unnumbered foes;
Let courage rise with danger
  And strength to strength oppose.

Stand up, stand up for Jesus;
  Stand in His strength alone.
The arm of flesh will fail you,
  Ye dare not trust your own.
Put on the Gospel armor;
  Each piece put on with prayer.
Where duty calls or danger,
  Be never wanting there.

Stand up, stand up for Jesus;
  The strife will not be long;
This day the din of battle,
  The next the victor's song.

The soldiers, overcoming,
  Their crown of life shall see
And with the King of Glory
  Shall reign eternally.

Prayer: Lord of Life, we thank you for the great reversal: Our sinful lives exchanged for your glory because of the death and resurrection of Your precious Son, Jesus Christ. Thanks be to You! Amen.

Lesson 10

The Shulammite Swept Up

You may recall our encounter with Solomon and the Shulammite in the last session. Take a moment now to review the words of Song of Solomon 6:8–9. Here we find a list of the other women in Solomon's life: sixty queens, eighty concubines, and virgins without number. Through political alliances, Solomon has amassed a harem. Is this what God intended? Are those who practice polygamy correct in saying, "God allowed this practice in the Old Testament, so society should accept the practice today"? By no means. Polygamy began after humankind's sinful fall. God's original intent for marriage is clear in Genesis 2, and the prescription for marriage is detailed in Ephesians 5. God established marriage as a divine union of one man and one woman for life. Polygamy had its origins not in the faithful descendants of Adam, but in his unfaithful descendants. It is Lamach, the offspring of Cain (the world's first murderer), who laughingly boasts, "Adah and Zillah, hear my voice; you wives of Lamach . . ." (Genesis 4:23).

What, then, of Solomon? His many wives led him astray to worship false gods. Over time, Solomon amassed a harem of 700 wives, princesses, and 300 concubines (1 Kings 11:3). And "Solomon did what was evil in the sight of the LORD" (11:6), "and the LORD was angry with Solomon, because his heart had turned away from the LORD, the God of Israel, who had appeared to him twice and had commanded him concerning this thing, that he should not go after other gods" (vv. 9–10). Although Solomon's love for the Shulammite prefigured Jesus Christ, we must remember that Solomon was a sinner. Only Jesus Christ was without sin. Out of His love for the world, Jesus endured the humiliation of the cross, making it possible for Christ and His Church to spend an eternity together. Christ is the One greater than Solomon (Luke 11:31).

Recognizing God's Gifts

122. At the close of last week's session, you were asked to comment on Martin Luther's belief that we should recognize God's gifts in other people. Do so now.

123. Discuss a time when someone honored God for the gifts He has given you.

The Shulammite Swept Up

Read 6:11–13.

124. From the Bible, we learn that Solomon made gardens and constructed parks during his reign (Ecclesiastes 2:5). The Shulammite journeys to one of those gardens to begin the sixth and final cycle of the couple's relationship (6:11–8:4). Why has the Shulammite come to this particular garden? What happens to the Shulammite while she is in the garden (6:12)?

125. What is significant about the Shulammite riding with Solomon in the royal chariot (consider Song of Solomon 6:8–10 as you answer)? What has she done to merit this experience?

126. How is this chariot ride another example of the great reversal theme found in Song of Solomon?

An Intimate Portrait

127. Following their chariot ride, we may assume that the couple retired to the privacy of their bedchamber. In 7:1–9, Solomon lovingly paints an intimate portrait of his "noble daughter" (v. 1), his dear wife Abishag, the Shulammite. We know that God crafted us in our mother's womb (Psalm 139:13). What interpretation could we make if we were to capitalize the word *master* in verse 1? What changes would we find in our marital relationship if couples realized their spouses were God's gift to them?

128. Song of Solomon 7:1–9 is unique in the Old Testament because it provides a portrait that is from "toe to head" instead of "head to toe." Compare this portrait with that found in 4:1–7. How do they both end? As you compare these two texts, keep in mind that 4:1–7 is early in the couple's married life, while 7:1–9 is later. What does this imply about their marital relationship?

129. Just as married spouses often do, the Shulammite finishes Solomon's sentence (v. 9). Now, read Song of Solomon 7:10. What does this lone verse say about the Shulammite's love for Solomon, and how do these words correspond to 1 Corinthians 7:4?

The Shulammite Gives Her Love

130. Read 7:11–8:4. How do we catch a glimpse of the Garden of Eden in this text?

131. Comment on the dynamics of marriage presented in this text. Discuss how this dynamic corresponds to 1 Corinthians 11:3 as well as the "creative order" established by God in Genesis 2:1–9, 20–24.

132. How does the Shulammite's desire for Solomon anticipate the Church's desire to be reunified with Jesus Christ (Revelation 22:1–5)?

133. For twenty-first-century Christians, the words of Song of Solomon 8:1 seem incestuous because the Shulammite wishes that Solomon was her brother so that she could kiss him; however, that is not the case at all. In ancient times, only close relatives were allowed to kiss one another in public. Even kissing by married couples was considered taboo outside of the privacy of their own home. In Old Testament times, only certain women kissed a man in public. Who were they (Proverbs 7:10–13)? Why does the Shulammite long to kiss her husband as her brother?

134. Explain the meaning of the adjuration found in 8:4. Where have we read these words before?

God's Word for Today

135. On earth, the Church seeks, finds, and anticipates its reunion with Jesus Christ at His second coming. In the meantime, the Church is sustained by her Lord until that blessed reunion. How does Christ

sustain His precious bride, the Church (Matthew 26:26–28; Revelation 19:6–9)?

In Closing

Encourage participants to begin the following activities:

- Compare Song of Solomon 8:6 with Ephesians 4:30.
- Discuss how we might consider 1 Corinthians 13:4–6 the Shulammite's (the Church's) creed.
- Read Song of Solomon 8:5–14 to prepare for the next session.

Speak or sing together the words of *Just as I Am, Without One Plea* (*LSB* 570:1–2, 6; *LW* 359).

Just as I am, without one plea
But that Thy blood was shed for me
And that Thou bidd'st me come to Thee,
O Lamb of God, I come, I come.

Just as I am and waiting not
To rid my soul of one dark blot,
To Thee, whose blood can cleanse each spot,
O Lamb of God, I come, I come.

Just as I am; Thy love unknown
Has broken ev'ry barrier down;
Now to be Thine, yea, Thine alone,
O Lamb of God, I come, I come.

Lesson 11

Yahweh's Flame

Daily, the entertainment world is aflutter with the latest superstar break-up or divorce. "Did you know 'so-and-so' were married only twenty-four hours before they decided to call it quits?" "We could see that divorce coming a long way off," another entertainment "guru" replies. God's powerful adjudication, to "not stir or awaken love until it pleases [God]," (8:4) pronounced by the Shulammite centuries ago falls on unheeding ears. Instead of relationships dedicated first to God and then to one another, love is awakened out of season (before marriage). The results are both devastating and tragic.

In contrast, the love of Solomon and the Shulammite is awakened at the proper time and within the bounds of holy matrimony. It grows and flourishes as a model for everyone to see. This is God's sacrificial love for the ancient Hebrews manifested in the lives of Solomon and his bride, the same love Paul reveals in his letter to the Ephesians (Ephesians 5:22–33). This is also God's love for you as lived out in Christ and summarized in the historic Apostles' Creed:

> [Jesus Christ] was conceived by the Holy Spirit, born of the Virgin Mary, suffered under Pontius Pilate, was crucified, died and was buried. He descended into hell. The third day He rose again from the dead. He ascended into heaven and sits at the right hand of God the Father Almighty. From thence He will come to judge the living and the dead.

Seeing the Church in the Shulammite

136. At the end of our previous lesson, you were asked to compare Song of Solomon 8:6 with Ephesians 4:30. Discuss your comparisons.

137. How might we consider 1 Corinthians 13:4–6 as the Shulammite's (the Church's) creed?

Love: The Flame of Yahweh

Read 8:5–7.

138. Some Bibles present verse 5a as a line delivered by "friends" or "they." Still others find verse 5a to be a continuation of the Shulammite's dialogue begun in 7:10. Regardless of who speaks this line, it is identical to 3:6a. To what major event in Jewish history do these two verses have their ties? Explain the symbolism found in these verses.

139. In 8:6 we learn of the Shulammite's desire for her husband manifested in an ancient practice in the Near East. What is the Shulammite's desire? How might the practice of exchanging rings during the wedding ceremony favorably compare with the Shulammite's desire?

140. When does God seal us with His grace, doing for us exactly what the Shulammite desired Solomon to do for her (Acts 2:38–39; Colossians 2:11–13)?

141. Who kindles the fire of love, a fire so strong that not even death can quench it (8:6)?

142. In the Bible, God sometimes attaches His presence to fire. In the Old Testament, God appeared as a "torch of fire" to confirm His

covenant with Abraham (Genesis 15:17–18). He appeared to Moses in the burning bush (Exodus 3:2), and He led the Israelites through the desert with a "pillar of fire" at night (Exodus 13:21). God's fire consumed the sacrifices offered to Him on the altar and then filled Solomon's temple with His presence (2 Chronicles 7:1–3). What New Testament event spotlighted in Acts 2:1–4 involved God's use of fire for Christ's apostles and disciples?

143. Listed below are some Scriptures substantiating the Shulammite's claim that love, ignited by God's grace, is stronger than death. Discover the circumstances behind each proof text and their meaning for your life.

- Genesis 3:15

- Genesis 7:11–13

- Exodus 14:29–31

- John 19:28–30

Seeking the Shulammite's Advice

144. In Song of Solomon 8:8–12, the "others" come seeking advice from the Shulammite. For whom are they concerned and what advice do they seek?

145. Where do you find the words of the Shulammite that support her virginity at the time of her marriage?

146. What advice is she giving to those who seek it? Examine and discuss the maturing of the Shulammite's love as it relates to verses 11–12 of our text.

147. The language of 8:10 provides an often overlooked wordplay. Take the time now to read it. Here the Shulammite speaks of finding "peace" in Solomon, whose name translates as "peace" in the Hebrew language. In a wonderful sign of His grace, God gave Solomon a second name at his birth (2 Samuel 12:24–25). Solomon's reign ushered in an unprecedented era of peace in Israel. Discuss the source of this peace if Solomon's nickname, Jedidiah, translates as "beloved of God."

Solomon's (the Lord's) Call

Read 8:13–14.

148. Through the mists of time, we can still hear Solomon's voice calling out to his wife as she converses with the "others" in his garden. How do his words show his deep affection for her? How does she respond?

God's Word for Today

149. Although undeserving of her husband's grace, the Shulammite responds to her husband as the Church does to the approaching second coming of our Lord. How are 8:14 and Revelation 22:20 similar?

150. The word *garden* appears in our text. This word alludes to the Garden of Eden. God's promise made in that ancient garden (Genesis 3:15) finds fulfillment in Christ's atoning death and resurrection and culminates in His second coming. What is this promise and how can we rightly say the great reversal is complete in Christ?

In Closing

Sing or speak together the words of *Lo, How a Rose E'er Blooming* (*LSB* 359:1–3; *LW* 67:1–2, 4). While singing this hymn, whose origins date back to the fifteenth century, recall how Jesus Christ is the bloom sung about here.

Lo, how a rose e'er blooming
From tender stem hath sprung!
Of Jesse's lineage coming
As prophets long have sung,
It came, a flow'ret bright,
Amid the cold of winter,
When half-spent was the night.

Isaiah 'twas foretold it,
The rose I have in mind;
With Mary we behold it,
The virgin mother kind.
To show God's love aright,
She bore to us a Savior,
When half-spent was the night.

This flow'r, whose fragrance tender
With sweetness fills the air,
Dispels with glorious splendor
The darkness ev'rywhere.
True man, yet very God,
From sin and death He saves us
And lightens ev'ry load.

Leader Notes

These notes are provided as a safety net, a place to turn for help in answering questions and for enriching discussion. They will not answer every question raised in your class. Please read them along with the questions before class. Consult them in class only after exploring the Bible references and discussing what they teach. Please note the different abilities of your class members. Some will easily find the Bible passages listed in this study; others will struggle. To make participation easier, team up members of the class. For example, if a question requires people to look up several passages, assign one passage to one group, the second to another, and so on. Divide the work. Let participants present the answers they discover.

Preparing to Teach Song of Solomon

To prepare to lead this study, read through the Book of Song of Solomon. You might read the introduction to the Song in the *Concordia Self-Study Bible* or a Bible handbook. Several maps of the city of Jerusalem, the united kingdom under David and Solomon's rule, and the ancient Near East at about 1000–900 BC would also be of great help.

If you have the opportunity, you will find it helpful to make use of other biblical reference works in the course of your study. These commentaries can be very helpful: Christopher W. Mitchell, *The Song of Songs*, Concordia Commentary (St. Louis: Concordia Publishing House, 2003); Roland C. Ehlke, *Ecclesiates/Song of Songs*, People's Bible Commentary (Milwaukee: Northwestern Publishing House, 1988; reprinted by Concordia Publishing House, 2004 [revised edition]); and Marvin H. Pope, *Song of Songs: A New Translation with Introduction and Commentary*, The Anchor Bible commentary series, William Foxwell Albright and David Noel Freedman, gen. eds. (New York: Doubleday, 1977) . Although it is not strictly a commentary, the section on Song of Solomon in *The Word Becoming Flesh* by Horace Hummel (St. Louis: Concordia Publishing House, 1970) also contains valuable material for the proper interpretation of this biblical book.

Group Bible Study

Group Bible study means mutual learning from one another under the guidance of a leader. The Bible is an inexhaustible resource. No one person can discover all it has to offer. The leader should resist the temptation to give answers and so act as an authority. This teaching approach stifles participation by individual members and can actually hamper learning. As a general rule, don't give interpretation, but try to develop interpreters. In other words, don't explain what the learners can discover by themselves. This is not to say that the leader shouldn't share insights and information gained by his or her class members during the lesson, engage them in meaningful sharing and discussion, or lead them to a summary of the lesson at the close.

Have a chalkboard and chalk or newsprint and marker available to emphasize significant points of the lesson. Rephrase your inquiries or the inquiries of participants as questions, problems, or issues. This provokes thought. Keep discussion to the point. List the answers given on the chalkboard or newsprint, then determine the most vital points made in the discussion. Ask additional questions to fill gaps.

The aim of every Bible study is to help people grow spiritually, not merely in biblical and theological knowledge, but in Christian thinking and living. This means growth in Christian attitudes, insights, and skills. The focus of this course must be Christ and the world of our day. The guiding question will be this: What does the Lord teach us about Himself and our life today through Song of Solomon?

Teaching the Old Testament

Teaching the Old Testament can degenerate into mere moralizing in which do-goodism becomes a substitute for the Gospel and sanctification gets confused with justification. Actually, the justified sinner is not moved by Law but by God's grace in Christ to a totally new life. His or her faith in Christ is always at work in every context of life. Meaningful personal Christianity consists of faith flowing from God's grace in Christ and is evidenced in love for other people. Having experienced God's free grace and forgiveness through the merits of Jesus, the Christian daily works in his or her world to reflect the will of God for humanity in every area of human endeavor.

Christian leaders are Gospel-oriented, not Law-oriented. They distinguish between the two. Both Law and Gospel are necessary because the Gospel will mean nothing unless we first have been crushed by the Law and see our sinfulness. There is no genuine Christianity where faith is not followed by lives pleasing to God. In fact, genuine faith is inseparable from life. The Gospel alone gives us the new heart that causes us to love God and our neighbor.

When Christians teach the Old Testament, they do not teach it as Law, but instead as books containing both Law and Gospel. They see the God of the Old Testament as a God of grace, who out of love establishes a covenant of love with His people (Deuteronomy 7:6–9) and forgives their sins. Christians interpret the Old Testament using the New Testament message of fulfilled prophecy through Jesus Christ. They teach as leaders who personally know the Lord Jesus as Savior, the victorious Christ who gives all believers a new life (2 Corinthians 5:17) and a new mission (John 20:21).

Pace Your Teaching

The lessons in this course of study are designed for a study session of at least an hour in length. If it is the desire and intent of the class to complete an entire lesson each session, it will be necessary for you to summarize the content of certain answers or biblical references in order to preserve time. Asking various class members to look up different Bible passages and to read them aloud to the rest of the class will save time over having every class member look up each reference.

Also, you may not want to cover every question in each lesson. This may lead to undue haste and frustration. Be selective. Pace your teaching. Spend no more than five to ten minutes opening the lesson. During the lesson, get the sweep of meaning. Stop occasionally to help the class gain understanding of a word or concept. Allow approximately five minutes for closing the lesson and announcements.

Should your group have more than a one-hour class period, you can be more leisurely, but do not allow any lesson to drag and become tiresome. Keep it moving. Keep it alive. Keep it meaningful. Eliminate some questions, and restrict yourself to those questions that are most meaningful to the members of the class. If most members study the text at home, they can report their findings, and the time gained can be applied to relating the lesson to life.

Good Preparation

Good preparation by you, the leader, usually affects the pleasure and satisfaction the class will experience.

Suggestions to the Leader for Using the Study Guide

The Lesson Pattern

This set of lessons is designed to aid Bible study, that is, to aid a consideration of the written Word of God, with discussion and personal application growing out of the text at hand.

The typical lesson is divided into these sections:

1. Theme Verse
2. Objectives
3. Questions and Answers
4. Closing

The theme verse and objectives give you assistance in arousing the interest of the group in the concepts of the lesson. Here is where you stimulate the minds of the class members. Do not linger too long over the introductory remarks.

The questions and answers provide the real spadework necessary for Bible study. Here the class digs, uncovers, and discovers; it gets the facts and observes them. Your comments are needed only to the extent that they help the group understand the text. The questions in this guide, corresponding to sections within the text, are intended to help the participants discover the meaning of the text.

Having determined what the text says, the class is ready to apply the message. Having heard, read, marked, and learned the Word of God, proceed to digest it inwardly through discussion, evaluation, and application. This is done, as this guide suggests, by taking the truths found in Scripture and applying them to the world and Christianity in general and then to personal Christian life. Class time may not permit discussion of all questions and topics. In preparation, you may need to select one or two and focus on them. Close the session by reviewing one important truth from the lesson.

Remember, the Word of God is sacred, but this study guide is not. The notes in this section offer only guidelines and suggestions. Do not hesitate to alter the guidelines or substitute others to meet your needs and the needs of the participants. Adapt your teaching plan to your class and your class period. Good teaching directs the learner to discover for himself or herself. For you, the teacher, this means directing the learner, not giving the learner answers. Choose the verses that should be looked up in Scripture. What discussion questions will you ask and at what points? Write them in the margin of your study guide. Involve class members, but give them clear directions. What practical actions might you propose for the week following the lesson? Which of the items do you consider most important for your class?

Consider how you can best use your teaching period. Do you have forty-five minutes? an hour? or an hour and a half? If time is short, what should you cut? Learn to become a wise steward of class time.

Plan a brief opening devotion using members of the class. Also, be sure to take time to summarize the lesson or have a class member do so.

Remember to pray frequently for yourself and your class. May God the Holy Spirit bless your study and your leading of others into the comforting truths of God's Christ-centered Word.

Lesson 1

Yearning for Love

Theme verse: *Let him kiss me with the kisses of his mouth!*

Song of Solomon 1:2

Objectives

By the power of the Holy Spirit working through God's Word, we will:

- discover the meaning of the Song's title, and then learn about its author;
- meet the Shulammite as she yearns for her marriage; and
- witness how God uses Solomon and the Shulammite to point us to Jesus Christ and His bride, the Church.

Setting the Stage

1. Answers will vary.
2. Answers will vary.

The Title and Authorship

3. Solomon sought God's wisdom so that he might govern God's people (the Israelite nation).

4. 1 Kings 4:29–43 teaches that Solomon possessed a "wisdom and understanding beyond measure," allowing him to compose 3,000 proverbs and write 1,005 songs. In addition, Solomon possessed knowledge of plants and animals, birds, reptiles, and fish. Solomon was wiser than all other men and his fame spread for miles around.

5. The proper name *Solomon* appears only a handful of times in the Song. Besides 1:5, we read it again only in 3:7, 9, 11; and 8:11. He is called king only twice more after the reference in 1:4 (1:12 and 7:5).

More common is the Shulammite's reference to Solomon as "my beloved."

Anticipation

6. She desires that her new husband would kiss her on the mouth (v. 2) and draw her near to him as she waits for him in the king's bedchamber (v. 4).

7. Scholars believe that the "she" mentioned in the pages of Song of Solomon is Abishag the Shulammite, whom King David married very late in life. She remained a virgin until she was married by David's son, Solomon, as he united David's kingdom. Additional background information on Solomon's feud with his brother Adonijah over Abishag's hand can be found in 1 Kings 2:19–25.

8. In John 14:2, Jesus promises that there are many rooms in His Father's mansion, which was a common phrase uttered by bridegrooms in ancient Near Eastern culture. 1 John 3:2–3 anticipates Christ's second coming (just as the Shulammite awaits the arrival of her husband, King Solomon). When Christ comes again, all believers will be made like Him. We anticipate that day with great joy!

9. Yes. The custom of anointing and perfuming the groom as well as the bride is suggested in verse three. As believers, we anticipate the second coming of Jesus Christ, who was anointed for the "great heavenly banquet" by Mary, who lovingly poured a pound of oil made from nard over Jesus' feet (John 12:3–7).

10. We learn that the Shulammite possessed a dark complexion, not unlike the curtains that hung between the Holy Place and the Holy of Holies in Solomon's temple (see Exodus 26:31). The Shulammite's tanned features may have come from tending grape arbors. The Shulammite's love compels her longing to be near him (Song of Solomon 1:7).

11. The Shulammite angered her brothers by not tending her vineyard (v. 6). Perhaps her love for Solomon is distracting her.

12. In Matthew 19:29, Jesus teaches that those who leave behind family or friends in their search for Him will receive a heavenly reward. This is what the Shulammite does; she leaves her vineyard untended because of her love for Solomon.

God's Word for Today

13. Paul speaks of this great reversal in these terms (Romans 6:23). Our sin deserves the punishment of death, but Christ died in our place so that we might receive eternal life instead.

14. Solomon tended God's sheep, the nation of Israel. In Matthew 12:42, Jesus calls Himself "greater" than Solomon. He is our Good Shepherd who "lays down his life for the sheep" (John 10:11). Jesus willingly sacrificed His own life that His sheep might live.

Lesson 2

The Bride Adorned

Theme verse: *Behold, you are beautiful, my love; behold, you are beautiful; your eyes are doves.*

Song of Solomon 1:15

Objectives

By the power of the Holy Spirit working through God's Word, we will:

- rejoice in the bride's beauty;
- learn about the many blessings God has showered on Solomon;
- discover the symbolism in Song of Solomon that points forward to the life, death, and resurrection of Jesus Christ; and
- compare the gifts Solomon showers on his bride to the gifts Christ bestows on His bride, the Church.

Who is this Bride?

15. When discussing what was gleaned from your Bible dictionary, be sure to focus on God's grace. God showed favor to Solomon not because of anything Solomon did, but that God's grace might shine and others come to faith. God was gracious to Abishag through Solomon. Solomon loved the Shulammite because God first loved him.

16. Answers will vary.

The Bride's Beauty

17. Solomon compares his bride to a mare among the Pharaoh's horses. Solomon imported horses from Egypt, which was well-known for producing the finest horses (1 Kings 10:26–29). Today, Solomon's

words may not seem to be a compliment, but they reflect a creature that is bold, proud, and majestic. As seen through Solomon's eyes, the Shulammite's beauty is unsurpassed. Solomon's word use also recalls a time when the proud Egyptian army found its match in God, who drowned them in the waters of the Red Sea, redeeming Israel and claiming her as His own.

18. A. bannered troops
B. fortified city wall
C. captivated Solomon

19. In 1:6, the Shulammite describes herself as deeply tanned because of the sun and asks that others not look at her. In 1:9–11, we see her prepared for her wedding, adorned and beautiful. We might call this the great reversal because she once considered herself unattractive but is now beautiful. Jesus Christ effected the great reversal for us by taking away the ugliness of our sin and by clothing us in His robe of righteousness in Baptism.

20. In Esther 2:12–13, we learn that, before a girl was admitted to the king's harem, she had to undergo twelve months of beauty treatments. These included six months of oil of myrrh applications and six months of perfumes and cosmetics.

21. As demonstrated through the Genesis account, "ornaments of gold" were provided by the bridegroom. The ornaments that adorn the Shulammite are gifts from Solomon placed on her by the "others." These "others" are most likely the "daughters of Jerusalem" who help prepare the Shulammite for her wedding day (3:10).

22. As Jesus relates in John 15:13–15, friends enjoy a special confidence that others do not. God created a special relationship between husband and wife. In marriage, a closeness exists like no other, for the husband and wife become one (Genesis 2:24; Ephesians 5:31).

23. The term of endearment the Shulammite uses in these passages is *my beloved.*

24. Mary anointed Jesus' feet with nard prior to His crucifixion, an act that showed her humility before the Lord and His teachings.

25. Myrrh was presented by the Wise Men who visited the baby Jesus (Matthew 2:11); it was offered as a pain reliever to a dying Jesus (Mark 15:23); and it was included in the mixture of spices brought by Nicodemus at the burial of Jesus (John 19:39).

26. Solomon's palace took thirteen years to complete. It measured a hundred cubits long, fifty cubits wide, and thirty cubits tall. Four

rows of cedar columns supported forty-five cedar beams. There were windows placed high in sets of threes; rectangular doors faced each other in sets of threes. Solomon made a colonnade measuring fifty cubits by thirty cubits with a portico featuring pillars and a hanging roof. There was a throne room constructed of cedar and living quarters of similar design. From this description, we can glimpse the magnificence of Solomon's temple and the significance of the great reversal. Solomon is providing everything to a woman who had nothing, just as God provides His riches to us at Christ's expense. That's grace . . . God's Riches At Christ's Expense.

27. The word *couch* and the Shulammite's reference to "cedar beams" indicate that the marriage consummation occurs in Solomon's private quarters within the palace.

God's Word for Today

28. Jesus declares and makes us holy through the gift of Baptism. The washing of Baptism makes us clean, without wrinkle or blemish. We are blameless and holy in His sight (much like the Shulammite in Solomon's sight as stated in Song of Solomon 1:15). Galatians 3:27 relates that Baptism clothes us in the righteousness of Christ (much as Solomon provided the adornments for his bride in our Scripture reading for today).

29. Through the help of the Holy Spirit, we seek to live lives that reflect Jesus Christ, who saved us from our sin.

30. Jesus Christ has redeemed us through His precious blood. The basis of this gift is not works on our part, but grace on His part. This is the great reversal.

Lesson 3

The Lily and the Apple Tree

Theme verse: *As a lily among brambles, so is my love among the young women.*

Song of Solomon 2:2

Objectives

By the power of the Holy Spirit working through God's Word, we will:

- discover the view the Shulammite has of herself;
- rejoice in how differently she looks to her husband, Solomon;
- learn the right time for love to be aroused; and
- compare the Shulammite to the Church, a lily among brambles.

31. Answers will vary. The roses mentioned in Song of Solomon may actually be the asphodel or even the narcissus plant. The nation of Israel has several varieties of lily, many of which were well known at the time Song of Solomon was written.

32. Answers will vary.

Inside the Bridal Chamber

33. The Shulammite compares herself to the roses and lilies growing in Sharon, a plain extending south from Mount Carmel along the Mediterranean coast.

34. With her references to roses and lilies, the Shulammite is comparing herself to common flowers. She is saying that there is nothing special about her appearance; she is plain and ordinary. Her words match 1:5–6, when she requests that others not look at her. She believes she is too ordinary to find favor in the eyes of King Solomon.

35. Solomon corrects her. She is indeed beautiful! Among other women, the Shulammite stands out as a lily among thorns. This mirrors Paul's comments in Ephesians, where he exhorts men to love their wives as they love themselves.

36. God's love for believers sets them apart in word and deed. At times of persecution, Christians also might appear as "lilies among brambles."

In Love's Embrace

37. Jesus says, "I am the vine; you are the branches" (John 15:5). What a wonderful way to describe how He sustains His Church with His Word (see Song of Solomon 2:3) until His second coming.

38. The Shulammite delights in her true love, Solomon. Answers will vary on the question of being close to one you love. The theological point behind this verse is that, as baptized believers, we long for the close contact with our Lord received through His Word and Sacraments. Ultimately, this longing will find fulfillment on the Last Day, when our Lord returns bodily and physically.

39. As previously discussed, our sustenance is provided through God's Word in the Gospel and Sacraments.

The Adjuration

40. An *adjuration* involves the swearing under oath to act or carry out a command given by another. In Song of Solomon 2:7, the Shulammite asks the daughters of Jerusalem to promise not to awake love until it pleases, swearing "by the gazelles or the does of the field." Wisdom literature often appeals to creation to teach the wisdom of the Creator, making this directive consistent with God's command (Deuteronomy 6:13).

41. The estate promoted in the Genesis and Matthew passages is marriage. Paul warns against sexual impropriety outside the bounds of marriage. As baptized believers, we are joined to Christ, and any sexual union outside the bounds of marriage is sinning against Christ's body. The Shulammite is adjuring the daughters of Jerusalem to restrain their sexual desires until they are married. Only then can sex be savored within the bounds and with the partner that God has provided them.

42. No, this adjuration applies to men as well. Peer pressure and media acceptance often lure young men and women into sexual

encounters that they one day regret, making the Shulammite's adjuration applicable today.

43. Consequences include unplanned pregnancy, social diseases, and broken families. Here are a few things that members of God's family may do to help prevent arousing love prematurely (perhaps you can think of others): serve as mentors to hold each other accountable for their actions, discuss God's desire for sex within the bounds of marriage in study groups, and teach abstinence until marriage.

God's Word for Today

44. Each time we take Holy Communion, we are reconnecting with Jesus Christ, the font of love. Although we are sinners, Christ comes to us offering His body and blood under the forms of bread and wine for the remission of our sins.

45. Each of these passages from Ezekiel highlights the Lord's desire that those who have sinned by awaking love before its time may come to Him, repent of their sin, and receive the forgiveness Jesus won for them on the cross.

Lesson 4

A Spring Marriage Proposal

Theme verse: *My beloved speaks and says to me: "Arise, my love, my beautiful one, and come away, for behold, the winter is past; the rain is over and gone."*

Song of Solomon 2:10–11

Objectives

By the power of the Holy Spirit working through God's Word, we will:

- view the courtship of Solomon and the Shulammite;
- compare this courtship with God's courtship of His Church;
- examine how God desires self-centered views to change through marriage; and
- discover how marriage can serve to reflect God's covenant with His people.

Anticipation

46. Answers will vary.

47. The universal Church waits in anticipation for the second coming of Jesus Christ as John details in Revelation.

48. The Shulammite compares Solomon to a gazelle or a young stag. Her comparison symbolizes agility and grace of movement.

Courtship

49. There are several indications in our text that we are viewing a period of courtship and not the couple's married life. First, Solomon is separated from the Shulammite and gazes at her through lattice (v. 9). Second, Solomon asks the Shulammite to come away with him, which

sounds very much like a marriage proposal (vv. 10–11). Third, we see that the Shulammite is inaccessible to him (v. 14).

50. Solomon's marriage proposal, repeated twice for us, is "Arise, my love, my beautiful one, and come away" (vv. 10, 13).

51. Notice the similarity between the two passages ("Awake, awake;" and "Arise") in Isaiah and that of Solomon in Song of Solomon 2:10, 13. In the parable of the ten virgins, Jesus teaches that we should always remain vigilant, for His second coming may occur at any time.

52. The most likely time of year for this proposal is spring, for the "flowers appear on the earth" (v. 12). Because the rainy season in Israel lasts from October through April, it is very likely this proposal occurs in May.

53. In Isaiah, we see God's promise of righteousness through the coming Messiah, who is Christ, the Lord. Through Him a sinful world will receive reconciliation.

54. Grapevines have long represented God's people. Jesus connects Himself to you and me today. Take a moment to examine His words in John 15:5. Foxes cause serious damage to grape harvests not only by their digging and nibbling the grape blossoms and later the grapes, but because fox urine ruins the soil. The jackals or foxes in our text are false prophets who would lead the Israelites astray. Are there foxes in the vineyard today? Discuss.

55. Yes, these two passages are saying the same thing. In marriage, couples no long exist as individuals, because the two become one. The reading from the Song and the reading from 1 Corinthians illustrate this point. Participants probably know of a marriage destroyed because the man and woman desired to remain individuals instead of becoming "one flesh" as God desires.

God's Word for Today

56. Through His covenants, God agreed to provide for His people. "Faithful human love that fulfills the First and Sixth Commandments is the fruit of God's love and God's fidelity to His Covenant of grace" (Rev. Dr. Christopher W. Mitchell, Old Testament scholar and CPH editor for the Concordia Commentary series).

57. God has sent His own dear Son to shine His light on the darkness of sin. This light serves as a beacon that calls those living in the darkness of sin to repentance and the forgiveness offered through the atoning sacrifice of Jesus.

Lesson 5

The First Nocturnal Search

Theme verse: *"Have you seen him whom my soul loves?"*

Song of Solomon 3:3

Objectives

By the power of the Holy Spirit working through God's Word, we will:

- learn how the love God has kindled drives the Shulammite to search for Solomon;
- relate the Shulammite's search to Mary Magdalene's search on Easter morning;
- discover the identify of the faithful helpers; and
- learn where we might find Him whom our souls love.

Lost Love

58. Answers will vary.
59. Answers will vary.

The Shulammite's First Nocturnal Search

60. These verses use different pronouns, which provides a clue on Solomon's and the Shulammite's dating relationship. Pronouns such as "my" (3:1) and "his" are common in describing a time prior to marriage when the self is most important. Those pronouns change to "our" as the relationship deepens in marriage and the two become one as God prescribes.

61. In 3:3, she calls Solomon "him whom my soul loves." She loves Solomon deeply, with her very soul (vv. 1–4). This is the same love we are to express toward God, because Christ commands us to

"Love the Lord your God with all your heart and with all your soul and with all your mind and with all your strength" (Mark 12:30). What comes to mind when someone says they love someone with all their soul? We think of the sacrificial love of Christ, who loved us so strongly that He went to the cross for our salvation, forgiving the times even when we are loveless.

62. On Easter Sunday, Mary Magdalene arrived at Jesus' tomb to find it empty. Running home, she reported the missing body to the disciples, who investigated and returned home. In despair, Mary wept. As she did, Jesus came and asked why she was weeping. Thinking Jesus was the gardener, she asked Him where they had taken her Lord. Only then did Jesus reveal Himself to her. For the Shulammite, love wakes her in the night to reveal that Solomon is not there, so she begins her nocturnal search. Areas of similarity include an almost frantic search for someone these women love dearly, disappointment at the end of their initial search, and the enlistment of someone to aid in their search (in the case of Mary Magdalene, the Lord Himself, while the Shulammite enlists the aid of watchmen). Each search came to a successful conclusion.

Faithful Helpers

63. The Shulammite began her search at night and she employed the city's watchmen to aid in her search for Solomon.

64. Ezekiel 3:17 and Isaiah 62:6–9 teach us that both of these men are prophetic figures responsible for the spiritual well-being of the Israelite community. Perhaps you can think of other men that God raised up for a similar purpose (e.g., Jeremiah, Jonah, Samson, Daniel, Micah, Habakkuk, etc.).

65. Pastors serve as our spiritual watchmen today. They are called and ordained into the Lord's service, charged with preaching and teaching God's Word in purity and truth as well as administering the Sacraments of Christ.

66. The Shulammite expressed a desire to consummate her marriage in the house of her mother. Scholars conclude that this phrase indicates that the Shulammite's mother supported her daughter's relationship with Solomon and that it stresses the Shulammite's high regard for her parents' marriage.

A Second Adjuration

67. The Shulammite's love for Solomon was so strong that it drove her into the streets of Jerusalem in search of him. However, her nocturnal quest could have been misinterpreted as that of a prostitute. (Such is the case in Song of Solomon 5:7. Such love should not be aroused for it can cause one to pursue their loved one with reckless abandon.)

God's Word for Today

68. God is warning us that a premature arousal of love may lead to disappointment and hurt. This warning often falls on unhearing ears in our society today. For those who do arouse love prematurely, God is steadfast and true, for He offers forgiveness to those who confess and believe in His Son (Romans 10:8–11).

69. We find the One "whom my soul loves" in His Word and the Sacraments of Baptism and the Lord's Supper. Our search for Him is always rewarded, because our search is begun by the power of the Holy Spirit, our Paraclete (Comforter or Advocate), who dwells within us and points us to the truth of Christ (John 14:15–17, 25–26; 15:26).

Lesson 6

The Wedding Day

Theme verse: *What is that coming up from the wilderness like columns of smoke . . . ?*

Song of Solomon 3:6a

Objectives

By the power of the Holy Spirit working through God's Word, we will:

- study the correlation between the Shulammite's wedding entourage and the exodus;
- learn about Old Testament theophanies;
- witness Solomon's grace toward the Shulammite and how that parallels God's grace; and
- learn what makes believers holy and blameless before God.

Your Wedding Remembered

70. Answers will vary.
71. Answers will vary.

The Wedding Procession and the Exodus

Begin by reading Song of Solomon 3:6–11.

72. In Exodus 13:21–22, God provided a physical manifestation of His presence (theophany) in the pillar of cloud that guided the Israelites by day and the pillar of fire that guided them by night. The Shulammite's arrival on her wedding day is compared to a column of smoke, similar to what we read in Exodus.

73. In Jeremiah, God refers to Israel as His bride. In Hosea, we find that God harkens back to the time when Israel came out of Egypt

and called Him "my husband." The entire sixteenth chapter of Ezekiel is filled with beautiful analogies, including the description of a wedding in verses 11–15. As we read the Ezekiel passages, we may almost envision the Shulammite, who came before Solomon with nothing, but now returns to him on her wedding day adorned in the finest fabrics and the most precious jewels. As Solomon adorned his precious bride, God adorned His chosen people with His mercy, making them holy and righteous in His sight. This anticipates Christ's perfect life and redemptive work on the cross. As believers, we are Christ's bride, made holy and righteous by His grace alone.

74. In Matthew 22:1–14, Jesus likens the kingdom of God to a marriage planned by a king for his son. As Christ's bride, we were purchased with a price (1 Corinthians 6:19–20), which was Christ's own blood (Revelation 5:9). Anticipating our royal wedding, Christ betrothed us and made us radiant, stain and blemish free, holy, and radiant in the waters of Holy Baptism (Ephesians 5:22–37). We look forward to celebrating His marriage to us in the great wedding feast (Revelation 19:6–10).

75. She is perfumed and dressed for her wedding and arrives in a carriage flanked by sixty fighting men armed with swords. This carriage was provided by Solomon and belongs to him (Song of Solomon 3:7).

76. Solomon arrives in an ornately decorated carriage made of cedar and overlaid with silver and gold. The seat he sits on is made of purple fabric. His head is adorned by the crown his mother placed on his head on his wedding day. Solomon's temple was also constructed of cedar and overlaid with precious metals and jewels decorated by master craftsmen. Solomon's arrival brings forth the image of the temple the Lord allowed Solomon to build.

77. The Shulammite enters in a fashion that is easily eclipsed by Solomon's ornate display. Likewise, believers will be eclipsed by the majesty of Christ when we see Him face-to-face.

78. Revelation 4:4, 10 present those in heaven as wearing crowns, while 3:11 seems imply that those whose faith rests in Jesus Christ already possess their crowns because of His redeeming work on the cross.

The Wedding Night

79. Solomon compares the Shulammite's eyes to doves behind a veil. Her hair is black. With Solomon's words, we can almost see the beauty of her hair as it bounces over her shoulders.

80. This order teaches that sexual relations are appropriate only within the confines of a marital relationship. Intercourse within marriage is in keeping with God's will, for only then is it pleasing in His sight.

God's Word for Today

81. In Paul's words, we find the ideal marital relationship. Here women submit (perhaps a better term is *surrender their will to their husband's*, as the Shulammite does in 7:10, which is best translated "I am my lover's; and over me is his desire"). Marriages would improve dramatically if each party in marriage treated the other with mutual respect and love. Paul announces that this is God's desire. In this sermonette, we see God's desire that men love their wives as Christ loved the Church; they should willingly give themselves up for their wives, if necessary.

82. Christ's righteousness, His perfect obedience to His Father's will, and His bitter sufferings and death are what make believers holy and blameless before God. In Baptism, these gifts of Christ are bestowed freely and are received through faith.

Lesson 7

Visions of Eden

Theme verse: *A garden locked is my sister, my bride, a spring locked, a fountain sealed.*

Song of Solomon 4:12

Objectives

By the power of the Holy Spirit working through God's Word, we will:

- review the differences between God and man before and after humankind's fall into sin;
- listen to the endearing words Solomon speaks to his new bride;
- compare the Shulammite to the Garden of Eden; and
- explore God's mercy through the "living water" of God's Word.

The Garden of Eden—Your Perspective

83. Genesis 2:24–25 places the pre-sin world before us. All of its countless riches are presented, including the creation of humankind. Note in verse seven that God gives man something no other creature has: a soul. Do you see the beauty of God's perfect creation? Trees, plants, and animals abound. The land is rich and fertile, yielding its crops in their season. All living things live in harmony with one another. We witness the creation of Eve, who is united with her husband in marriage as pronounced by God (Genesis 2:24).

84. The differences are obvious. Harmony no longer exists between God and humankind. Sin is a wedge driven deeply between the two. As marital relations are concerned, there is no peace either. Husbands and wives strive for personal achievements, forgetting the purpose for which God created them. They are no longer of one flesh,

but two personalities at odds with themselves and God. Only through Christ's unifying grace can husband and wife live as God desires (Ephesians 5:21–33).

Another View of Solomon's Proposal

85. Most likely Solomon spoke these words at the Shulammite's mother's home when he proposed marriage to her.

86. Through poetic verse, Solomon is proposing that the Shulammite marry him. This passage recalls the actions of Moses, to whom God gave a glimpse of the Promised Land (Deuteronomy 34:1–4).

At the Altar

87. Solomon continually calls the Shulammite "my bride." In Isaiah 62:1–5, God says that He will rejoice over Israel as a bridegroom rejoices over his bride. What a wonderful preview of Christ's rejoicing at His second coming when He welcomes those whom He has declared righteous.

88. Solomon describes his wife's kisses as dripping with nectar and her breath as sweet as honey and milk. The passages from Exodus and Joshua refer to the Promised Land as it was described during the time of the exodus: a land flowing with milk and honey.

89. Another term of endearment used by Solomon is "my sister" (4:9–10, 12; 5:1–2). Solomon also uses other terms throughout this Song, some of which we have examined previously: "my love" (1:9, 15; 2:2, 10, 13; 4:1, 7; 5:2; 6:4), "my dove" and "my perfect one" (2:14; 5:2; 6:9), and "my beautiful one" (2:10, 13).

The Locked Garden

90. "A garden locked, . . . a spring locked, [and] a fountain sealed" indicate that the Shulammite has saved her virginity until her wedding night. Christ has sealed us in our Baptism, marking us as redeemed by His precious blood. In a sense, in Baptism He restored our spiritual virginity (1 Corinthians 6:11; Ephesians 5:25–27).

91. The other garden is the Garden of Eden, which God closed off after Adam sinned to prevent him from eating from the tree of life and living forever in his sin. For believers, paradise comes again at Christ's second coming.

92. While Jesus connects "living water" to the Holy Spirit in John 7:38–39, in this passage the "living water" He offers the woman is eternal (v. 14). The Holy Spirit, working through the Word of Christ, imparts eternal life through God's Word.

93. In marriage, our bodies no longer belong to us alone, they belong to our marriage partner as well.

94. They encourage the newly married couple to drink deeply of the love they have for each other.

God's Word for Today

95. In Acts, we learn that the Lord calls us to repentance followed by the reassurance of eternal life in Christ. In Ephesians, we hear of God's good and gracious will; through Baptism we are cleansed of our sins and declared holy and blameless.

Lesson 8

Second Nocturnal Search

Theme verse: *I sought him, but found him not; I called him, but he gave no answer.*

Song of Solomon 5:6b

Objectives

By the power of the Holy Spirit working through God's Word, we will:

- distinguish between the two parts of this section: dream and reality;
- learn God's wonderful promise to those who seek Him;
- contrast the actions of the watchmen with those witnessed earlier; and
- rejoice in God's Gospel message to those who remain faithful in times of suffering.

Changes and Conflict

96. Answers will vary. Be aware that some participants may feel uncomfortable answering this question. Tell them that they need not discuss personal matters involving their marriage or give specific names. They may speak in generalities, if they desire.

97. Answers will vary. Be aware that some participants may feel uncomfortable answering this question. The desire is to discuss the relationship in a general, or even anonymous, way so that feelings are not hurt and participants are not offended.

The Dream

Read 5:2–8, then answer the following questions.

98. The opening words of our text indicate that the Shulammite is asleep and dreaming: "I slept, but my heart was awake" (Song of Solomon 5:2).

99. In 3:1, she refers to him as "him whom my soul loves," while in 5:2 she calls him "my beloved."

100. The one term of endearment Solomon leaves out is "my bride." The relationship between Solomon and the Shulammite is changing as they mature in their marriage. Relationships change over time.

101. She has readied herself for bed; her daytime garments are removed and she has washed her feet in preparation for rest. In Luke 11:5–8, Jesus speaks of a man who has retired for the night when a friend arrives asking for food to feed a guest in his home. At first the man refuses, but later he opens the door to his friend.

Reality and the Search

102. The Shulammite awakens to find Solomon gone. In reality he was never there.

103. Each of these women felt lost and alone because the one they loved was gone.

104. Through Isaiah 65:12, we find God using the language of Song of Solomon 5:6 to call His rebellious people back to Him. God promises that all those who seek Him will find Him (Isaiah 65:1).

105. In 5:7, the watchmen beat the Shulammite and chastised her for walking the streets. This action stands in sharp contrast to the action they took earlier when they offered to help her find Solomon.

106. Ancient watchmen were responsible for the morals of their community as well as guarding the city from intruders. In the case of the Shulammite, the watchmen may have mistaken her for a prostitute, chastised her, then removed her veil. Perhaps this is why we never hear the Shulammite seeking revenge on the watchmen. Most likely they were just doing their duty.

Another Adjuration

107. This adjuration is addressed to the daughters of Jerusalem and today's society as well. The Shulammite's adjuration that they tell Solomon that she is lovesick shows what can happen when one is in love. Here love caused the Shulammite to dream that Solomon was at her door. It drove her into the streets in search of him when, in reality,

he was never there. This is the love that must not be aroused unless one is married, because it is so powerful that it causes things to happen beyond our control. Only the presence of Solomon can cure her lovesickness.

God's Word for Today

108. In these three verses, we learn that, although the Church is persecuted during the time of separation from her Lord, He has given us the Holy Spirit to comfort and guide us until the hour of His second coming.

109. Paul teaches us that suffering is good because it produces in the believer a hope of things to come, an eternity with God. What a wonderful Gospel message: we who are forgiven sinners are joined with Christ's death and in Baptism are raised to new life (Romans 6:3–8).

Lesson 9

Christ and His Church Prefigured

Theme verse: *His arms are rods of gold, set with jewels. His body is polished ivory, bedecked with sapphires.*

Song of Solomon 5:14

Objectives

By the power of the Holy Spirit working through God's Word, we will:

- unveil a portrait of Solomon;
- discover how this portrait relates to Jesus Christ as king and priest;
- compare Solomon's portrait with the images of Christ found in the Old and New Testaments; and
- thank God for His gift of undeserved grace.

Digging a Little Deeper

110. Descriptions will vary.

Christ Prefigured in Solomon

111. The daughters of Jerusalem respond to the Shulammite's request for help by asking for details on Solomon's appearance. They also want to know what makes him different so they might recognize him when they find him.

112. The Shulammite's intimate portrait includes his features, which she says are radiant and ruddy. Solomon's head is like gold; his hair is black. He has "eyes . . . like doves" and cheeks of spices and

lips "dripping liquid myrrh." We also glimpse Solomon's strength: his "arms are rods of gold, set with jewels;" "his body is polished ivory" with sapphires. His skin is white, for the Shulammite refers to Solomon's legs as the color of alabaster firmly planted on a base of gold. He stands erect as do the cedar trees in Lebanon. In total, Solomon is "altogether desirable" (v. 16).

113. Images of a king: "head is the finest gold" (v. 11). Most likely Solomon wears a crown. Images of a priest are found in the references to jewels and sapphires (v. 14), because each was used in the breastplate worn by the high priest (see Exodus 28:18, 20; 39:11, 13). Images of the Garden of Eden are in the Shulammite's references to gold, jewels, and sapphires (v. 14) for these precious commodities were found there (Ezekiel 28:13).

114. In each case, we view the image of a radiant man unlike any other. Perhaps you have read the Synoptic Gospel accounts of Christ's transfiguration before, but have not set them beside the accounts found in the Old Testament books of Ezekiel, Daniel, and Song of Solomon. Long before Christ was transfigured, God gave Solomon, and the two prophets Ezekiel and Daniel, a look into the future with a precious glimpse of their Savior, Jesus Christ.

115. The Shulammite speaks of gold and jewels (some translations say *tarnish*, as yet an unknown jewel), as well as sapphires. All of these substances were extremely valuable, as were myrrh and ivory. Like the answer to question 113, the time of the exodus is recalled in the gold, sapphires, and jewels. These commodities were part of the high priest's breastplate, on which were inscribed the names of the twelve tribes of Israel (Exodus 39:8–14). Regarding the future, the apostle John mentions that these precious objects are part of the new Jerusalem when Christ comes again in His glory.

116. We are ransomed by Christ's precious blood. Our faith is built on the Living Stone, Jesus Christ.

Solomon's Location

117. The daughters of Jerusalem asked where the Shulammite thinks they may find Solomon. In their asking they honored both the Seventh and Eighth Commandments. They wanted Solomon and the Shulammite to love and honor each other in their marriage, so they honored God by working to bring them together. They also honored

God by not enticing away their neighbor's husband, but instead urging the couple to stay together.

118. By inverting the phrase "my beloved is mine, and I am his" (2:16) to "I am my beloved's, and my beloved is mine" (6:3), we see that the Shulammite's focus is maturing in marriage. No longer does she think of herself first; she thinks first of her husband. What differences would we find in marriage if all couples focused on their marriage partner instead of themselves? Selfishness can easily dismantle even the most carefully-built marriage. The specific examples cited will vary.

The Shulammite: Christ's Church Prefigured

119. Solomon compares the Shulammite to the other women in his life (6:8), but still considers her his "dove," his "perfect one." (We will discuss polygamy in the beginning of our next lesson.) Solomon also mentions that his other queens and concubines praise the beauty of the Shulammite (v. 9).

120. The words "bright as the sun" carry a theological meaning. In his letter to the Galatians, Paul defines what is meant by Solomon's words: The Shulammite, like Christ's Church, shines with the glory Christ has given her. The Church is clothed in His righteousness. We also see another example of Solomon's esteem for his wife in words found earlier in verse 10. Here Solomon says she is as beautiful as the moon, pointing to the lofty position she holds over all the other women in his kingdom.

God's Word for Today

121. God has rescued us from our sin through the precious blood of His only Son, Jesus Christ. Just as the Shulammite was elevated to a lofty position by her husband, we are elevated to eternal life through God's own Son.

Lesson 10

The Shulammite Swept Up

Theme verse: *Before I was aware, my desire set me among the chariots of my kinsman, a prince.*

Song of Solomon 6:12

Objectives

By the power of the Holy Spirit working through God's Word, we will:

- unlock the significance of the Shulammite riding in the royal chariot;
- recognize that our spouses are God's gift to us;
- discover the uniqueness of the Shulammite's description found in Song of Solomon 7:1–9; and
- learn how Jesus Christ sustains His Church on earth.

Recognizing God's Gifts

122. Answers will vary. Be sure to note that we often take God's precious gifts of our family, friends, associates, and spouses, for granted.

123. Answers will vary.

The Shulammite Swept Up

124. The Shulammite has come to inspect the garden. She is looking for blossoms, the harbingers of fruit. While she is in the garden, Solomon comes and sweeps her into his chariot.

125. A ride in the king's chariot indicates the Shulammite's lofty status as Solomon's "dove" and "perfect one." With great pride,

Solomon shows off his beautiful wife. The Shulammite has done nothing to merit this experience.

126. Her deep tan from working outside in the vineyards made the Shulammite feel undesirable (1:5–7), and yet Solomon's love for her literally "sweeps her off her feet," landing her in Solomon's chariot. This reversal of fortune can be due only to grace; it points to an even greater reversal accomplished for us through our Savior, Jesus Christ.

An Intimate Portrait

127. By capitalizing the word *master* in verse one, we attribute the creation of the Shulammite (as well as all humankind) to God. When we consider our spouses as God's gift to us, we elevate them to the same lofty status as Solomon gave the Shulammite. In response to such a precious gift from God, with the help of the Holy Spirit, we would willingly keep God's mandate given in Ephesians 5:21–33.

128. Both end with an expression of Solomon's desire to consummate their marriage (4:6; 7:8–9). The marital relationship between Solomon and the Shulammite remains strong and each desires to express their love sexually, partaking of the intimate joy God has provided for them.

129. Song of Solomon 7:10 demonstrates the maturity of the Shulammite's love for Solomon. We see that above all else she desires to please him. Her body no longer belongs to her; it belongs to her husband (see 1 Corinthians 7:4).

The Shulammite Gives Her Love

130. This discourse includes references to vineyards, grape blossoms, pomegranate blossoms, and the fragrant smell of mandrakes, harkening back to the beauty of God's lush paradise in the Garden of Eden.

131. In 7:11–8:4, we witness the Shulammite's desire that Solomon exercise his headship over her (1 Corinthians 11:3). She belongs to her husband and willingly submits to his will as was established in the "creative order" presented in Genesis. God ordained that the man should "head" (guide both physically and spiritually) the family with woman as his helper. Notice that 1 Corinthians 11:3 goes on to say that a man is head of the family; Christ is head over man. 1 Corinthians 11:3 dovetails Paul's words in Ephesians 5:28–30, where

we are told that, while a man is head of the family, he is to treat his wife with self-sacrificial love and honor just as Christ loves the Church.

132. Revelation 22:1–5 opens the curtain on an eternity spent with God. No longer will we live under the curse of sin (Revelation 22:3). We will see God's face (Revelation 22:4). As Christians, we long to spend an eternity with God, a longing we can rightly compare with that of the Shulammite's longing for Solomon.

133. In Old Testament times, only a prostitute kissed a man in public. The Shulammite loves Solomon so much, she wishes the entire world could see the expression of her love and faithfulness.

134. Again the Shulammite pleads with the daughters of Jerusalem not to waken love until it pleases God, and that is only within the boundaries of marriage. We have seen this same adjuration on two other occasions (2:7; 3:5). The repetition of this theme serves to emphasize its importance. In this case, God wants us to know of His desire that we not awake this love until it is within the setting of a marital relationship.

God's Word for Today

135. The Lord Jesus Christ sustains the Church on earth by feeding it His own body and blood offered in the Eucharist in anticipation of the great wedding feast (Revelation 19:6–9).

Lesson 11

Yahweh's Flame

Theme verse: *Love is strong as death, jealousy is fierce as the grave. Its flashes are flashes of fire, the very flame of the LORD.*

Song of Solomon 8:6

Objectives

By the power of the Holy Spirit working through God's Word, we will:

- contemplate how Song of Solomon ties to the exodus event;
- learn about God's symbolic use of fire in both the Old and New Testaments;
- examine the advice the Shulammite gives regarding marriage; and
- rejoice that Jesus Christ fulfilled God's promise in Genesis 3:15, completing the great reversal.

Seeing the Church in the Shulammite

136. In Song of Solomon 8:6, the Shulammite desires that Solomon set her as a seal around his arm; a metaphor for what Jesus Christ does for us (Ephesians 4:30). The blood of Jesus Christ seals us to Him for eternity.

137. By God's grace, the Shulammite's love conforms to the characteristics laid out in 1 Corinthians 13:4–6. You may recall that the Shulammite put Solomon's will ahead of hers (Song of Solomon 7:10).

Love: The Flame of Yahweh

138. The major event alluded to in our text is the exodus. Here, God led the nation of Israel out of the wilderness as a pillar of cloud by day and a pillar of fire at night (Exodus 13:21–22).

139. The ancient practice of wearing a seal is noted in this text. In those days, a seal was commonly worn as a cylinder about the neck or as a bracelet or ring. This allowed the wearer to mark his or her seal of authority into wet clay. Later, seals were stamped into sealing wax. What the Shulammite desires is that Solomon wear a seal attesting to his spiritual connection to her by his grace. In modern times, such a "sealing" is attested by the exchange and wearing of wedding bands, which favorably compares to the Shulammite's desire.

140. In Acts, we learn that believers are sealed at their Baptism, a pronouncement confirmed in Colossians 2:11–13.

141. Yahweh, the God of Abraham, Isaac, and Jacob, and the Father of our Lord, Jesus Christ.

142. The giving of the Holy Spirit at Pentecost when the disciples saw what appeared to be tongues of fire alight on them.

143. Genesis 3:15 previews of the highpoint of God's love in the promise of a Savior to redeem the world back to Him. In Genesis 7:11–13, we see God's love shown in the rescue of Noah and his family during the time of the great flood. Exodus 14:29–31 shows God's love in the rescue of His people through the parting of the Red Sea. John 19:28–30 is the fulfillment of God's redeeming love, with the death of Jesus Christ as the atoning sacrifice for the sins of the world.

Seeking the Shulammite's Advice

144. They are concerned with protecting the chastity and fidelity of their little sister.

145. The Shulammite's phrase "I was a wall" in 8:10 supports that she was a virgin at the time of her marriage to Solomon. This statement also adds credibility to the notion that the Shulammite is Abishag (1 Kings 1:1–4).

146. The advice that the Shulammite gives is that she remained a virgin until the time of her marriage, so she encourages the "others" to follow her example. We witness another example of her marital maturity when she confesses that she has a vineyard that produces a thousand pieces of silver that she willingly gives to Solomon. In marriage, when spouses commit financial deception, it can cause

problems. Solomon and the Shulammite have become one in their marriage, just as God directs.

147. In Solomon's nickname we see an acknowledgement of God, who is the true source of all peace.

Solomon's (the Lord's) Call

148. Chapter 8, verse 13 speaks of Solomon's desire to hear his wife's voice because he loves the Shulammite so deeply. Married spouses often experience a desire to hear the voice of the one they love. The Shulammite responds to her husband's call by requesting to see Solomon again in words that remind us of their courtship (2:9).

God's Word for Today

149. As the Shulammite hurries to be near her husband, the Church replies with the words often expressed between the two advents of our Lord, "Come, Lord Jesus," because we long for our reunification and an eternity spent in our heavenly Bridegroom's presence.

150. The promise in Genesis 3:15 is that God would one day provide a Savior who would deliver His people from their sin. At His death, Jesus Christ atoned for all sins, forever. In Baptism, undeserving sinners are clothed in Christ's righteousness and presented to the Father as the bride of Christ. This truly is the great reversal. In Christ's second coming believers will depart to live with God and Christ forever. Amen. Come, Lord Jesus!